PARABLES
FOR THE
PRESENT

PARABLES FOR THE PRESENT

Christine Fleming Heffner

HAWTHORN BOOKS, INC.
Publishers/NEW YORK

With thanks to Kenneth and Norton
and a group of other people
who have all given important pointers
to me

Contents

Introduction		xi
1	The View from a Teapot	3
2	Gifts and Wrappings	6
3	The Homesick King	9
4	Power, Success, and Fame	11
5	Proof	13
6	Fool for a Patient	17
7	Dunkirk	21
8	The Mixed-up Library	25
9	God's Lessons	28
10	Scrapping the Obsolete	30
11	The Bankrupt	32
12	Black Light on the Congregation	35
13	Hill on the Horizon	38
14	A Handful of Light	40
15	Addiction	43
16	Wrong Gear	46
17	When the Band Plays	48
18	Truth and a Nickel	50

19 *Supercargo*   52

20 *Translation*   55

21 *The Parish Bake Shop*   59

22 *Human Algebra*   61

23 *There's a War On*   63

24 *What God?*   65

25 *The Sick Man*   67

26 *No Deadheads*   70

27 *Perfect Understanding*   71

28 *Lamps*   73

29 *Who's Behind the Wheel?*   75

30 *Need Glasses?*   77

31 *Symbols*   80

32 *Who Is Strong?*   82

33 *Point of View*   84

34 *Getting Ready*   86

35 *From Missouri*   89

36 *The Simple Gospel*   92

37 *A Leaf and Elisha*   94

38 *The Empty Pew*   96

39 *Eye on the Target*   98

40 *Counterfeits*   100

41 *Crutches in the Chapel*   103

42 *After the Horse Is Gone*   106

43 *Fellow Travelers*   108

44 *Which Daughter?*   111

45 *Looking for God*   114

46 *Pueblo and Project*   116

47 *Dollars and Delphiniums*   119
48 *The Blue Garden*   122
49 *Fence Straddlers*   124
50 *Emergency Room*   126

Introduction

The minute hand on the alarm clock isn't much of a thing. It may be plain or fancy, but all it really is is a stick. A stick that points to something. That is what a parable is, too —a verbal stick, in plain language or elequent rhetoric, but all the same a stick that points to one thing.

There is an idea around that parables were invented along with and specifically for the Bible and that they don't belong anywhere else. The truth is that men probably used parables almost as soon as they began to use words at all, and they certainly didn't stop using them when they finally gathered together the library they put into one book and called the Bible. As a matter of fact, you are very likely to miss the points of the biblical parables if you think they are so terribly special that you have to treat them with a lot of reverence. When you are too much in awe of the parable itself, you may be looking so hard at the pointer that you don't see what it is pointing at, looking so hard at the minute hand that you don't know whether it is five minutes after the hour or ten minutes till.

So—a parable is like a minute hand, which won't tell you

what day it is or what month it is, but you probably know those things anyway. It won't even tell you what hour it is, but if you don't know that, you might be able to guess. A minute hand is likely to tell you what you haven't found out for yourself or what you haven't noticed. Use it for what it is meant.

Bookstores are usually loaded with volumes that offer you somebody's philosophy, his way of living with himself and with other people. Some of these are good philosophies and can be helpful, but the fact is that most of us have to work out our own philosophies for ourselves, from our own experiences, from what we are told by teachers we trust, and, above all, from our own relationships with the God who created our lives in the first place. In other words, most people really know what month it is, and if they don't know the date, they know how to find it out. The reason they need a clock is to find out just what time it is and whether or not they have time to do this before they have to do that. If your flight leaves at seven-forty and your watch doesn't have a minute hand to point out where you are between seven and eight o'clock, you may well miss the plane.

And back to the alarm clock: If the minute hand isn't there, the clock may not go off, in which case you might not wake up when you need to.

The author and publishers of this book hope you will use its parables as minute hands, pointers to the little things that can have such big consequences in life. Minutes are little things, but so are medicines, so are habits and happinesses, so are words and the elements of wisdom.

PARABLES
FOR THE
PRESENT

1

THE VIEW
FROM A TEAPOT

⋞§§⋟

These days we seem to live surrounded by earthshaking events, by cataclysm, death, and destruction, by riots, assassinations, and wars. This, we are told ad infinitum (as if it were not already obvious to us) is an age of crisis. Civilization is at the crossroads. In truth every age in man's history has been an age of crisis, and civilization has stood at some kind of crossroads since before the first wheel turned. No matter—it is certainly true that there is nothing tranquil, stable, or reassuring about the time we live in.

For most of us, however, it is really not the world-shattering events that make our lives what they are. The things that deprive us of the joy, love, and liberty we yearn for are seldom the affairs of nations. Rather, they are the little strifes and discords of our daily living. The storms of war, for all the terrible havoc they can mean to us, don't affect our eternal destiny as much as the tempests in our own teapots.

Look back at the broken friendships you have known, the personal enmities, the bitternesses, the angers and despairs.

How often do their real sources lie in matters of great moment? How few marriages are severed over matters of principle? How terribly many are shattered by things that weigh fluff-light in the scales of human history, even less in the scales of eternal values!

Most of the things that disturb us are trivial, yet our eternal destiny may hang on them rather than on our true griefs, our real tragedies, just because we do give these minor things more import than they deserve.

It is exceedingly dangerous to live in a teapot. Any imprisonment is a dreadful thing, but this self-imprisonment can be the worst there is in loss of freedom. The fate of nations doesn't even matter to the man in a teapot. He hardly notices nations. For that matter he hardly notices the people he lives with. There is no room in the teapot for anyone but him, as there is not room in his mind or his heart for anything more than himself. Certainly there is no room for love. Love is too huge a thing, even in its tiniest manifestations, to be crammed into any life that only exists from one small personal tempest to the next.

Why do people waste away their lives in teapots? It isn't comfortable there. It is cramped, and there is no room at all for growth. It is stuffy there, and the very narrowness keeps a man raw and touchy. Not much light can find its way into a teapot, so it's a gloomy kind of life. Though it is secure in a way, even its security is shallow and false. Still, once you get used to living in a teapot, you cling to the false security of confinement, afraid to lift the lid.

Looking up the spout of a teapot, you can see so little of

4

life. You can see even less of God. All you can see of the Cross and the Resurrection, all you can see of your Church, are details: the nails, but not the Hands; the altar, but not the Bread; the people in the next pew, perhaps, but not the Communion of all the Saints. You can't make out the meaning of what you do see, and you can never know the power of it all.

The great danger about life in a teapot is that if you choose, you may stay there—forever. You can curl up in the teapot like Alice's dormouse, and the teapot, even with its little exciting tempests, becomes your spiritual grave.

But of course you can climb out, if you are willing to.

2

GIFTS AND WRAPPINGS

◆§※◈

Gift-wrapping has become a whole industry. Not only can you buy pretty paper and ribbon and cards suited to any probable occasion, and a few improbable ones, but you can buy gadgets to help you make bows and roses and such ornaments to put on the packages. You can even buy the ornaments already made up, if you don't want to bother doing it yourself.

Then there's the paper for the outside wrapping. The first wrapping is far too pretty and too expensive to leave unprotected, so you have to wrap *it* up. There are sticky tapes to seal packages with. Some of them even have little wires or cords embedded in them so that no one, not even the recipient, can possibly open the packages they are used on.

Pretty wrappings are fun. They make getting a present more exciting, and they build up the anticipation involved in opening a gift. Sometimes they build it up so high that by the time you manage to open the box all you have is a letdown.

That's what life sometimes hands us, too—packages all wrapped up in shiny foil and satin ribbon, decorated with sequins and sparkles, but containing nothing but a penny whistle, and that's broken.

The gifts of God are different. Some of His wrappings are pretty glorious, too, but when they are you can bet the contents are even more glorious, so don't ever leave His gifts wrapped up, just admiring the packages. Most of His gifts seem to come in modest packages, but the presents themselves are always splendid just the same.

Some of His gifts come to us in nothing more than a brown paper bag and turn out to be beyond price and beyond description. (How can anyone possibly think that God doesn't have a sense of humor?)

If you don't know the Giver, then you might stick brown paper bags and beat-up boxes away to open later. You're in more of a hurry to open the shiny packages that promise so much. But if the paper bag gets forgotten, you may never find the gift that waits inside.

Oh, lots of the things He offers us are gift-wrapped. He sends some in the rich colors of stained glass and organ music. Some He wraps in the glitter of rapture, and some He ties with the gold cords of romance. But not many. It seems to be that the very best gifts of all are the very ones He sends in the plainest wrappers. Love, for instance, really comes wrapped in something very like the daily newspaper and is tied up with responsibilities. Courage is bundled up in a package of fear and strain. Even a thing like joy may come wrapped, strangely enough, in heartbreak. And if you ever envy others the gift of faith, be sure you haven't got it stuck away somewhere in a corner, never taken out of its package of self-distrust and disillusion.

In the end the wrapping doesn't count; it's the gift that matters. What the gift is depends on the giver. We get more excited over a gift from a close friend than we do over one from a casual acquaintance. The friend loves us, knows us, and knows what we want. When the gift is from God it is from One who loves us more than we can imagine and from One who knows us even better (indeed, far better) than we know ourselves. It is from One who knows perfectly not only what we want but what we need.

When He doesn't give us what we want (or at least what we think we want), we still may be sure that He is giving us instead the things we badly need, and we are ignoring them because of their wrappings.

Life keeps offering glamorous packages. God keeps giving gifts wrapped any old way. Forget the satin ribbon and cellophane. It's the Giver that really matters.

3

THE HOMESICK
KING

᪣

You can find a lot of truth in fairy stories. Somewhere in a children's fairy story there lived a prince who had been kidnapped as a child and raised in poverty. When he was grown, someone identified him and he succeeded to the throne.

What happened after that isn't important, except that the young king who now had everything he could possibly want was miserable. He ruled an empire, yet he was frustrated. He had every comfort, yet he suffered.

That's the story of our life. Here we are, we human beings, rulers of nature. There are hurricanes and volcanos and earthquakes, but by and large man has remarkable control of his environment. He has sufficient control of it to be able to destroy it, and he may do just that. He's dug out some of nature's most awesome secrets and put his knowledge to work making himself more and more powerful over the world he lives in. Man is ruler, yet he's frustrated. He is the most powerful animal on earth, yet he feels strangely weak.

He can manage just about every natural thing except himself.

Man should be reasonably comfortable. He has food and lodging available. He can cool the air around him when the temperature is higher than he likes and can warm it when the cold would hurt him. When it's dry, he can humidify his surroundings, and when it's too wet for comfort, he can dry out the atmosphere. He can do a lot to relieve pain. He can cure many diseases and even prevent some of them. But he suffers. Oddly, he seems to suffer most deeply when he is most comfortable.

What's the matter with man, anyway? Statistics show that in the very places where he never had it so good, he is most likely to commit suicide. In places where he has the greatest sources of ease and pleasure, despair pervades his arts.

What is the matter with man? He is homesick. Rulership, comfort, and pleasure combined cannot cure his nostalgia. No matter how much he gussies up the palace, it isn't home.

St. Augustine said that God has made man for Himself and that man's heart is restless unless it can rest in God. Many other wise and holy men have said the same thing in other ways.

Whenever you hear somebody talking about man's progress in taking over the management of the universe, remember what man is. He's a homesick king, and he never will enjoy being a king very much. He may not be aware of it, but he'd really much rather go home.

He can go home—that is what the Christian Good News is.

4

POWER, SUCCESS,
AND FAME

ఎప్రిపా

When Harry left the party with a few under his belt, every-body said he wasn't drunk. He was just feeling good. There are a lot of things that can make you feel good, and some of them are worse in their effects than alcohol, worse even than the most poisonous drugs.

Power is one of them. A little power is an awfully com-fortable thing to have. You don't even need to throw it around. Just knowing you have it makes you feel good. You know that others can't upstage you, and the best part is that they know it too. If you don't get your way when you think you should, you don't have to persuade anybody of anything. Just push a little.

Success makes you feel good, too. Maybe that's because there is power in it, but there's more to it than that. Success means that you don't have to doubt yourself anymore. You have it made. You *know* you're good. So you don't have to improve, grow, bend, change. You can just sit there, fat, dumb, and happy on your laurels.

Fame is like success, only more so. You have more people telling you how good you are.

Of course, pleasure makes you feel good. That's what it's for. The trouble is that we get to thinking we are made for pleasure instead of pleasure being made for us. Pleasure makes you feel so good you can forget everything else—even the things you need to remember.

Harry wasn't drunk. He was just feeling good. But after a while his car was going a little faster than he usually drove it and his reactions were a little slower than they usually were, and then he didn't feel good anymore. He didn't feel at all. Neither did somebody in the other car.

Power and success and fame and pleasure can work the same way. They can, indeed, be the death of us (which *might* be our own business, though you'd have to face some pretty powerful arguments on that). The point is that our power and fame and pleasure can be the death of somebody else. You never have a right to risk that.

Alcohol is fine in its place. Its place is not the bloodstream of a person who is carrying responsibility. Power is fine in its place, too. It's the only way to make a society run. Even success and fame are fine in their places, and pleasure has its perfectly legitimate uses.

Just remember that they're all loaded. Even in small quantities.

5

PROOF

❦

A lot of people think that any knowledge can only be the result of proof——I mean algebraic proof or laboratory proof. Real scientists who work to establish that kind of proof seldom think this, but ordinary laymen, who have been told so often that they are the products and inhabitants of a scientific age, still sometimes do.

Some kinds of knowledge do have to come from objective demonstration of some kind, but not all. It depends on the kind of knowledge; it even may depend on what you already know.

You can use algebraic proofs in order to establish some things. You look at all the elements involved, you put them into logical order, and if you really do have all the factors and your logic runs straight, you have your proof. You write Q.E.D. Or do you? You may have omitted a factor of which you are simply unaware or your logic may have a twist in it. What you really have is not so much proof as it is hypothesis —a theory that looks to be true.

Certainly that method can't be used to prove, for example, that a medicine will work. For that kind of knowledge you must resort to the laboratory. Even to begin to achieve valid laboratory proofs you have to work with what are called controls. Controls are the negative attempt, the same conditions and the same process without the factor you are adding to be tested. Controls are the way you try to have it both ways. If you don't have rigid, and usually secret, controls you can't be sure that your test factor was responsible for the outcome of the test. The same results might have come anyway. There might be some other factor you are not taking into account. (The real scientists are actually thoroughgoing agnostics about their own work.)

If you are trying to prove that a drug cures a certain disease, you give it to some subjects who suffer from that ailment and you also give something that looks like it but isn't to some others. If those who received the drug improve and the ones who got the imitation do not, then you have the proof of your drug. Probably. Even this kind of proof is not quite *that* simple.

This kind of proof, however, is just not possible when you deal with the kind of knowledge you must live by. You can't ever try a decision both ways. All your life you keep having to decide what to do without the help of a laboratory —often without the help of logic.

Sometimes you can work out this kind of knowledge by trial and error, in the way that you find out which key fits a lock. If the door opens when you turn the key, it fits. Of course, the errors can be costly and painful.

But go further—into the pain and price of the errors. Sometimes the worst thing you can have happen is to find that the key does fit and the door does open—and it was the wrong door, more like Pandora's box than the entrance you were looking for. The proof may be a proof, all right, but you get lost in the problems of what it proves. You've got knowledge, all right, but not the kind you want. A lot of people have gotten themselves that kind of knowledge about alcohol, sex, drugs, and living for the sake of kicks generally. There can be useful, helpful knowledge of all these things, but there can be disastrous knowledge of them, too, and ignorance is no more to be regained than innocence.

Sometimes a lock in your life just doesn't have a key at all. It seems that if there is any way of opening it, it must be by a combination. You could never guess that combination and you know that you won't live long enough to try it every possible way. Then you can only get your knowledge from somebody else, somebody who does have the combination, and you have to take their word for it. If you think they may know that combination, you'd better ask them.

What you really want isn't proof at all. It's help. Because we live in a scientific age, we think in terms of proof about things that are outside the realm of science, things that are outside the area of proof. In that meaning Christianity is one of these things. You cannot prove it algebraically, that is, by logic. It isn't logical, and has never claimed to be. You can't prove it by the laboratory kind of experiment, trying it both ways—you have to commit yourself. You can't find any kind of worldly key to it. You have to take the word of one who knows. Well, God came to earth as man to give that Word—He *is* that Word—for each of us. He is the only one who really can give us answers where we are looking for some kind of proof we can handle. He is the key, the only one, to the important locks in our lives. He is the Way.

God has the combination to living as a real human being, and He has made it clear to us. He has given it to you. Then the only way you can *prove* it is to use it.

6

FOOL FOR A
PATIENT

⋖᠗⋗

Everyone knows that doctors don't usually treat their own families, except in emergencies. Some people even think that there is a law against their doing so. There is no such law; doctors don't treat their families because they know that toward their own kith and kin they cannot be sufficiently objective to be sound and effective, either in diagnosis or therapy.

Sometimes a physician who wouldn't think of treating his wife or his son undertakes to treat himself. This is an even more dangerous undertaking, because no man can be objective about himself at all. He is too close.

Once a physician (and a good one) made this mistake. It was such a simple matter: He was taking antihistamines for an allergy and he did his own prescribing. When he finally diagnosed his brain tumor he went to a fellow physician. But there wasn't any brain tumor. Though his symptoms were identical to those of a brain tumor, they were the simple result of a severe and continued overdosage of antihistamines

—a larger dosage over a longer period of time than that physician would have ever thought of allowing any of his patients.

There is an old saying that the lawyer who takes his own case has a fool for a client. The doctor who treats himself has a fool for a patient, and he also has the world's worst physician. He can't diagnose his own illness no matter how learned he is. He can't prescribe his own treatment wisely no matter how high his professional standing. Toward himself he will be either too easy or too hard. If he is too easy, he will pass off even serious symptoms as trivial and will take the treatment that is comfortable. If he is too hard, he will panic over minor disabilities and prescribe impossible therapy. In either case he would be better off under the care of the nearest druggist or his mother-in-law.

No man can be his own spiritual physician either. He can't keep his inner life healthy on his own judgment, no matter how mature and wise he may be. We are all biased in our own favor. Some of us are so much so that we expect the superhuman from ourselves and will settle for nothing less. Either we excuse ourselves however bad our case or we drive ourselves no matter what we accomplish. Our serious spiritual symptoms seem trivial if we want them to be trivial; our minor shortcomings can seem critical if we are too proud to put up with our own humanness. Only an outsider can tell us the whole truth about ourselves. Only an outsider can tell us what kind of treatment we need to make us healthy.

We are like the mother whose child holds a drawing up at the end of her nose—we're too close to focus.

Through the ages Christian spiritual physicians have been diagnosing and prescribing for spiritual ills just like our twentieth-century ones. Even the Old Testament prophets speak very much to our condition because there are few, if any, really modern ills of soul and character. Mostly you and I suffer from the same old spiritual colds and flu and pneumonia, hangnails and headaches, cataracts and cancer from which men have always suffered. If we were more familiar with the Christian classics—especially that Christian classic *par excellence*, the Holy Bible—than most of us are, we would recognize that our situation, even when it is grave, is hardly unique.

Familiarity with the writings of our spiritual ancestors could also help us to recognize our symptoms enough not to treat them for ourselves but to know whether we ought to make a leisurely appointment with the doctor or call the rescue squad. At any rate they could serve us as a kind of "what-to-do-till-the-doctor-comes" for the soul.

We've grown up not thinking about souls as being ill because we didn't think about souls, period. Most of us haven't had spiritual training enough to apply a bandage, much less a tourniquet. Christians of some other times have been more fortunate. They knew how to help one another in spiritual emergencies and where to find professional help.

The Christian classics make clear what sin is, whereas most modern so-called religious books either ignore the subject or deny it. The classics outline the fundamentals of spiritual discipline, including the discipline of exerting toward ourselves the same charity that is demanded in our dealings with others. They not only set up standards against which to measure spiritual health, they give advice in attaining it. Most of them sound surprisingly contemporary in their subject matter if not their syntax.

The Church has always been meant to be a spiritual hospital (complete with outpatient clinic, of course) and our pastors are meant to be our spiritual physicians, to diagnose our illnesses and prescribe treatment. But the Church cannot serve *us* as a hospital if we don't recognize that we are ill and need its help; our pastors cannot diagnose or treat us if we assume there is nothing wrong with us and expect nothing of them but the conduct of regular services and the oversight of the parish affairs. Christian tradition stands behind our parish church and our pastor, ready to teach us the fundamentals of sound spiritual nutrition and exercise, but it can do nothing for us if we see tradition as nothing more than a collection of heirlooms and ourselves as spiritually healthy when we are not.

We run-of-the-pew Christians need to make use of the helps offered by the Church in its worship and its teachings; in its dedicated, trained, and often inspired manpower; in its traditions; and in the unbiased counsel of our spiritual directors. As long as we try to diagnose and treat ourselves we shall only get worse.

7

DUNKIRK

◦§◦

Dunkirk is one of those loaded place-names such as Marathon, Waterloo, and Pearl Harbor. The name of the place became the name of an event, and the event has meaning far beyond either that time or that place.

Dunkirk, victorious defeat. Dunkirk, a massive miracle of rescue worked by the ordinary, everyday people who are the soul and fiber of any nation. Dunkirk, the place where the men who manned the little pleasure boats and fishing craft of England took their place in the history of man's courage and resourcefulness.

This was a major battle, utterly lost. Here the best remnants of a nation's fighting forces were driven to the sea, with no fleet at hand to rescue them from disaster. Because it was a black hour for that army in that stage of that particular war, it was a black hour for the very cause of liberty.

Then, out of the disaster came the miracle. From across the Channel came the boats—not ships but boats—manned by fishermen and clerks, gardeners and executives. Here were prosaic little Englishmen who wore no uniform and dreamed of no glory, shipping little workaday boats and little bouncing pleasure craft across a Channel most of them were never meant to sail, to do, in danger by sea and by air, one of the most glorious pieces of fighting in the history of heroes. It was not the kind of battle that flies flags and blows bugles, but it was the kind of battle that wins lost wars, this labor and pain and danger undertaken by free men in order that their brothers might be saved from the adversary who had overwhelmed them.

Dunkirk was the place where hope arose out of defeat. It was the place where the weak and common things of the earth were used (as they often are used and as the Bible has promised that they will be used) to confound the mighty. Little boats, little men, neither fit for battle—but they rescued their beleaguered fighting men from a victorious force.

Sooner or later to every man there comes a Dunkirk. There comes a time when his soul staggers to the edge of destruction, overcome by the enemy, exhausted, cornered, desperate.

When that happens, then it is that all the little boats of that man's life can come to the rescue of his threatened will. Some are the little workaday boats, the little habits, disciplines, sacrifices of his everyday life, the traits and characteristics that are his from hour to hour in his home or his office. Some are pleasure craft, the little kindnesses and honesties, the disciplines acquired in his hours of rest and play. They are all little boats he never dreamed were important, small craft that had nothing to do with danger or temptation. Yet here they come, able and willing in time of peril to rescue him from an enemy that seems already to have proved too strong for his resources.

Such little boats cannot conquer his enemy by themselves, but they can bring him out of disaster; and from the shelter of that rescue he can gather strength to face the enemy again and defeat him. The knowledge of the little boats that support him can be to his morale then what the little boats of England were to the British Army. Once they have come to his need, he knows forever after that they stand behind him.

What if those little boats are not there? What if they have fallen into bad repair; what if they are unseaworthy? What if there is no one to bring them to him? What if there are no little habits, minor disciplines, small sacrifices, daily honesties to come to his aid? Then his disaster must be final.

Little kindnesses cannot come to the aid of a man's love when he has neglected too many chances to be kind. Daily honesties cannot bolster his integrity when he has too often fallen back on little lies. Minor self-discipline cannot strengthen his will and his courage when he has too often chosen self-indulgence. Vision and insight are lost to the man who has taken the path of self-justification, of rationalization. Fresh supplies of moral stamina will never come to the man who has leaned on too many crutches, taken too many escapes in the trials, pains, and disappointments of daily existence.

This is the way life is. This is why God is so concerned with everything a man does—with his passing pleasures and daily tasks as much as with his great crises and grave temptations. This is why Jesus said, "He that is faithful in that which is least is faithful also in much" (Luke 16:10) for He knew that the weak things in life exist to confound the strong and that it is the way a man lives from moment to moment that will decide how he survives in a critical hour.

Jesus the Christ is not, as we sometimes think, One who comes to us in our hour of peril; rather, He is One who stays with us all through our common hours—unless we choose to keep Him out. It is His use of the little boats we have already let Him pilot that can turn a defeat into a Dunkirk for us. It is the little boats we keep away from His hand that can leave us to catastrophe.

8

THE MIXED-UP
LIBRARY

ক্ষুই

One Halloween, somebody got into the library and mixed up the books. He put all the Bibles and religious classics and the lives of the saints in the section marked "Science." He put all the books on scientific and technological subjects and industry into the section marked "Religion."

As a Halloween prank, maybe it was fairly original, but the idea has been around for a long time, and people have been mixing up their own libraries in just that way.

For a while they used to look in the Bible for scientific mistakes, find them, then throw out the whole works. Occasionally some scientist would announce the accuracy of some biblical reference and then the people who wanted to believe in the Bible would think that perhaps they could after all. But mostly the believers had to be pretty much on the defensive.

The detractors would begin with Genesis: How could the world have been created in six days when for part of that time there was no sun by which to measure days? Sheer logic read the whole thing out of court at the start. (I recently read a learned scientist's guess that the universe took millions of years to be formed and I wondered how *he* measured years, but that is beside the point.)

Now, however, the problem is mostly the other way around. People turn to the scientific section of the library, are impressed by the massive knowledge in the fields of science and technology (all of which they just call "science"), and try to live their lives by what the books on those subjects say. You can find a lot more self-contradiction in this section of the library than you can in the religion section, but it doesn't seem to bother many people. This is a scientific age (or we keep being told that it is) and a lot of people feel that we must try to live scientifically. Science is supposed to tell us how to love, for instance, and how to be honest, and the difference between right and wrong (or that there isn't any); it is supposed to explain how to live with our consciences and families, with our enemies and ourselves.

Real scientists don't usually claim to have the key to these things. They know that finding out the weight of a star doesn't tell you how it came to be, that knowing the number of chemical elements in a man's body doesn't tell you very much about the man, and that knowing biology doesn't help you much in achieving a good marriage.

The Bible begins at the beginning (right there with Genesis where the detractors boggled) to show that this set of writings is about God and about man. It isn't about the things that science deals with: weights, quantities, dates, and distances. You will never learn much geography, geology, biophysics, or botany from the Bible. You were never meant to. Equally you cannot learn much about living from a physics textbook or even a book on biology. You aren't meant to do that either.

If you look to a scientific treatise for a recipe telling you how to live, you will not only mess up your life, you will also miss the beauty and richness that scientific knowledge cannot give you. If you look to the Bible for scientific information, you'll not only wind up scientifically ignorant, you will miss learning how to live.

9

GOD'S LESSONS

࿐

All our lives, whenever we set out to learn something, we find that most of that learning is achieved by doing. We may first have to commit to memory some basic principles, but soon we are busy using them, at first awkwardly, crudely, then with increasing skill. We learned arithmetic by doing sums; we learned our native language (and others, if we are lucky) by speaking and reading.

Yet we always seem surprised to find that we must learn spiritual lessons in the same way. We learn to worship God by joining others in praising Him. We learn to believe and trust in Him by having to use the belief and trust we already have. Humility is the first and last thing most of us need to learn and we learn it by being knocked by life from one humbling experience to another.

Maybe you have been missing some of the lessons you need to learn just because you don't recognize the drill involved.

Would you learn patience? Exercise it on the next bore who afflicts you.

Would you learn gratitude? Look around you and give thanks.

Would you learn diligence? Pitch in to do and do well the tasks that lie in front of you.

Would you learn hospitality? Open your heart (though not always your door) to all who knock.

Finally, would you learn love? Indeed, you must learn love if you are to learn God's lessons at all since this skill is central to being a functioning Christian. The only way to learn it is to love, and love, and love.

10

SCRAPPING
THE OBSOLETE

❧❦❧

Long ago and far away a nation's defense department (or whatever its bureaucratic equivalent) developed a new kind of weapon. It was more effective than the old crossbow or whatever it was with which that nation's fighting forces were armed. It seemed that with the new equipment the nation might at last be able to fend off its strongest enemy.

"Away with the crossbow" was the watchword, and all the thousands of crossbows were burned, while the metal parts were melted down for horseshoes or doorlatches. So the obsolete crossbows were scrapped. And the enemy attacked.

That nation went down in utter defeat because while the crossbows were being scrapped the wonderful new weapon was still on the drawing board. It had actually never been built.

Sometimes Christians seem to be like that nation. "Away with the Ten Commandments," they say. "They're negative. They're obsolete. The Christian Summary of the Law is greater and stronger and much more effective. We'll use the law of love and then we won't need any Thou-shalt-nots to run our lives by." Out go the Ten Commandments; out go the Thou-shalt-nots. The world, the flesh, and the devil attack.

But where *is* the Summary of the Law? Still in the Book? Where is its commanded total love for God, love that takes *all* of a man's strength, *all* of a man's heart, *all* of a man's soul? Where is any real love of neighbor, when the first and fundamental love of God is missing? Where is the self-discipline that the law of love demands? Where is sacrifice? Where is the wisdom that love of neighbor must require?

The Ten Commandments have been scrapped, all right, but there isn't anything Christian about doing that: It is obedience to the Summary of those same Commandments that is the Christian replacement, the Christian law. If you don't live by either the Ten or the Two that are their summary, then your enemy wins, with ease.

11

THE BANKRUPT

Willis owed everybody in town, they said. He didn't really owe everybody, but he did owe a lot of people a lot of money. Since he went further into debt every year, he finally went bankrupt. His creditors got about twenty cents on every dollar he owed them.

Willis was such a nice guy. He'd give you the shirt off his back, they said. That wasn't quite accurate either, but he did give money to every charitable cause that came along. When they took up a collection at the office for somebody who had an accident and everybody else put in fifty cents, he put in a couple of bucks.

Everybody said it was such a shame about Willis going broke. Look at all the pennypinchers who never give a nickel to the needy and yet who prosper themselves. Well, it wasn't really *everybody* who said this. It seemed to a few people that if Willis owed that money he didn't really have it to give. As one of the typists put it, it wasn't really Willis helping all those good causes, it was his creditors.

Most of us know a Willis, a guy whose vaguely good-natured instincts make his irresponsibility look more like generosity than it really is. He's a great guy to know if you want to make a touch, but not much of a friend if *he* has touched *you*.

There are good lives that are like that too. There's the woman who spends so much time doing volunteer work that her children are raised by the neighbors. There's the man who gives his time and intelligence to a home for the aged, and whose mother hasn't heard from him in months. There's the man who is on every committee in his service club while his wife raises their children by herself. The world is full of people who spend what they owe to Peter so they will look good to Paul (and to themselves).

Our whole society is like that, really. The concern for the individual, the works of compassion for the poor and incapable, the great charity hospitals, and the aim for education for all—these things we point to as "our way of life" mostly have their origins in Christian teachings and Christian practice. But Christian teachings demand some other things besides, things we don't consider part of our way of life at all.

Democratic principles existed before Christ, but then nobody intended them to apply to every man. The idea that the weak should be defended by the strong is a heritage from the age of chivalry, which for all its imperfections in practice was Christian in principle. We tend to say, "Look how generous we are," without looking to see where our generosity came from.

We take credit for the things we spend our lives doing; we

forget God, who created that life. We grow in self-esteem when we use our heads and our hands for the sake of others; we give little thought or labor to God Himself, who made the hands and the heads, the brains and the muscles. Finally, we give a little love away and we feel like saints; but saints are people who remember that all love is from God and is due to Him and that we can only truly love at all because God has loved us.

Individuals give away what is owed to God and wonder why they finally go bankrupt. Society gives to men and forgets God and wonders why it is so empty.

12

BLACK LIGHT
ON THE CONGREGATION

◆§◈◈

"Black light" may sound like a self-contradiction, but it is the common name of ultraviolet light, the light that you can't see but *by which* you can see things that disappear in ordinary visible light. Your nearest museum probably has a display in which you push a button, the light shining on an array of ordinary-looking rocks goes off, and suddenly in what seems to be no light at all some of the rocks glow with varying colors and others are picked out in streaks and blobs of brightness.

Every Sunday morning someone writes into the records of each church the size of the congregation, but the usher or clergyman who counts the house does it by ordinary light. He counts the people he can see. For record-keeping purposes this is necessary, but in an important way it is misleading. The figure in the book is never the whole truth about the size of the congregation. In the black light—if one might call it that—of reality the house-count may be very different indeed.

To begin with, there are people in the pews, people who get counted for the record who do not show up in the black light. When the daylight of our everyday way of looking at things is turned off, these people just disappear. You can't see them in the darkness of eternity, that darkness that today's light will become once today is past. As early as tomorrow the presence of these people will be without effect, so, eternally speaking, even today really only counts their absence. These are the people who come to church without really coming, people who send only their bodies, perhaps even their social and official selves, but send nothing that is warm or loving or groping or desiring or even hating or sinning—nothing of themselves that is in any way *alive*.

Now you must not for a moment think that you know who these people are: Only the black light of eternity shows up their absence, and neither your eyes nor mine can yet see by that light. If they could you might be surprised. The silly, dithering matron; the stiff old *dame formidable*, who frowns at an intruder in "her pew"; or the banker whose church-going seems so much a conventional part of his conventional being—any of these may turn out to shine with a far brighter glow than you do! How *they* look in that light is no affair of yours. Your only concern is whether or not *you* are visible.

Then there are the empty pews, empty to the official eye, that is. In the black light of everlasting reality they may not be empty at all. They may be jammed, not only with Christians who have achieved everlasting reality wherever it is that the merely here-and-now is no more and the eternal is all there is; jammed not only with those messengers of God who have always played a greater part in your and my eternal reality than we guess; but also full of all who would like to be there and cannot, those whose hearts and hopes and faith are there though their bodies are somewhere else, perhaps in hospital beds and wheelchairs.

Count the house? For the record, yes, because the church's business in this world must be done well if it is to do well its eternal business. But remember the purpose of those statistics; don't push them beyond their proper application. The real success of a parish church or a clergyman cannot be satistically proven. The Lord of Hosts has made it pretty clear that He is unimpressed by numbers. He is concerned for each rather than with all. The record of the ages seems to show that He tends not to count men but to weigh them.

13

HILL ON
THE HORIZON

◄§§►

In the rare, dry atmosphere of the southwestern desert, distances are deceptive. There used to be a little train, one car carrying baggage and passengers, that ran once a day through a part of Arizona's Gila Valley. Perhaps it still runs, and perhaps it still stops sometimes at Fort Thomas. The fort, then, was a crumbling ruin on a largely uninhabited plateau between two mountain ranges. Perhaps it has all crumbled away by now, but the train didn't stop because the fort was there but because there were, on the highway that ran alongside the track, a few houses and a filling station that boasted a few shelves of canned groceries.

There is a story (and the people who lived there claimed it was true) that once, when the train stopped at Fort Thomas for some needed repair, an easterner went off for a little walk. He had been told that it would be at least two hours until the train could go on its way and he was restless.

Three hours later, when the train was ready to proceed, the man had not come back. In fact he didn't get back for two days and was much worse for wear when he did. Accustomed to hikes through his own countryside, he had thought to take a stroll to the foot of Mount Turnbull, a single peak that looms some seventeen miles west of Fort Thomas and stands out dramatically against the jagged horizon. In that deceptive air Mount Turnbull looked close enough for a brisk walk; in that landscape directions can be as deceptive as distances.

Sometimes Christianity is like that mountain. It looks so close because we are so familiar with it. Because it seems nearer than it is, it looks smaller than it is. It appears but an easy stroll from wherever we happen to be, and it looks as though it would be a simple climb when we get there. Christianity is a lot bigger and a lot further away than you may think. Be sure that it is no mere hill that you can run up in order to get an inspiring view of the sunset. It's no place to stroll to while you wait for something else.

14

A HANDFUL
OF LIGHT

✥

Tommy came into the living room in his pajamas, weeping bitterly in rage and frustration. Tommy had made an experiment and it had failed.

Tommy had simply tried to carry some light from the hallway into his bedroom, but no matter how tightly he clutched the light in his hand, by the time he opened it there was only darkness. Tommy was, of course, very young. People with an experimental turn of mind learn frustration early.

Tommy's father explained that light couldn't be carried that way but that it could be moved around if you carried the source of it. He took a flashlight into Tommy's room and showed him how to turn it on and off, and Tommy was so charmed with the flashlight that he forgot his frustration, which was probably what Tommy's father had in mind.

Tommy had learned a lesson that a lot of grown-ups never learn. Some people try to carry the light of Christianity into the world as Tommy tried to carry light into his room—

in their own hands. They work very hard trying to carry the compassion and self-sacrifice that have shined in this gloomy world from the Star of Bethlehem and the Easter dawn and the flames of Pentecost, but they don't carry the source of that light, Christ Himself. No matter how tightly they clench their hands around the light, they find only their own darkness when they want to lighten the darkness of others.

These are the people who try to get Adam and his children to love their neighbors without knowing about, much less loving, God. Their hands are opened freely but the light has disappeared, and Adam keeps on hating his neighbors.

These are the people who labor at improving the sorry lot of miserable men by providing better housing, better clothing, more education. But even when the miserable men get their minds crammed with technology and sit in good houses, dressed in good clothes, they are still miserable, because they don't have the answers to their basic problems, their uniquely human problems. You can fill stomachs with nutritious food and heal sickness with wonder drugs and still leave men hungry, still leave their spirits sick. Full minds can live with empty hearts and often do. Basic darkness can brood on in the midst of learning and dignity and plenty. The light, carried that way, carried so painfully, so earnestly, never reaches the places where it is intended to shine.

These are the people who honestly think it doesn't matter what a man believes, that all that is important is the way he lives. You might as well say that candles and lamps and electric wires, or even eyes, are not important, that the only thing worth bothering about is light itself. Goodness, justice, and compassion are the fruits of a belief, not the basis for one.

We who have for so long been the beneficiaries of Christianity often have forgotten where our light comes from. As a society we have come to take the light for granted, because we never quite wholly knew darkness, but neither a society nor an individual can have light unless it has access to the source of light. We cannot carry the light of Christ in our brains or in books or in techniques or in good works, any more than we can carry the hall light in our hand. Nor can we borrow a cupful from a neighbor when we grow afraid in the dark.

You can't have light and you can't shed light unless you get it from its source. You can't have Christianity, you can't have saints, without Christ. You and I can't banish darkness from the earth, no matter what we spend in money, labor, or learning. Only Christ can do that. We *can* carry Him in our minds, our hearts, our wills, into our society, into our world. If we do, then the food, the houses, and the medicine will come. However, those things will not bring the beauty and warmth and safety that men need; they will not erase fear and evil. The Son of God Himself must accomplish that. That is the only way it can be done.

Like Tommy, we cannot just carry the light in our own hands.

15

ADDICTION

❧

If you are like most people who have no contact with alcoholism or drug addiction (and these people are fewer than one might suppose), you react to either subject with ambivalence. You may feel sorry for the addict or the drunk, but all the same you have a feeling that they don't need to be that way. After all, you have problems, too, and you don't resort to a needle or a bottle.

Don't be too smug. Maybe you've never so much as taken an aspirin. You still may be an addict, and the only difference between you and the "mainliner" may be that your way of running away from yourself is respectable.

Even as common a thing as eating can be an addiction. All right, so eating is necessary to life, and if we are healthy we enjoy it. But overeating can be an addiction. People who don't like life the way it is may take comfort in eating to help erase the hurt of being alive—which is, very roughly, why the alcoholic drinks or the addict takes heroin or whatever else he uses to make him be someone he isn't. Of course, drug addiction—or alcoholism—is not that simple, and there is an all-too-real physical entity involved. But overeating is not that simple either. They come close enough to be worth some long, hard, face-the-music thinking—and not while you drink a milk shake.

You are underweight? Don't close the subject. Perhaps your addiction is to overtalking. Most people talk too much when they are tired, or bored, or ill at ease. Some people talk incessantly, frantically, at any time, or they talk so they won't have to listen, or they talk in order to build up the egos that have to have top place or make their owners miserable.

A particularly virulent kind of overtalking is the addiction to complaint. The incessant complainer, the total whiner, doesn't want sympathy. Indeed, nothing will make him worse as quickly as getting sympathy. Complaining as a way of life goes deeper than that, deeper even than self-pity. It's a crutch. It's an escape from facing life. It's a weapon against the world. While nobody much likes a complainer, nobody dislikes him as he does himself.

In the urban, twentieth-century United States, probably the most common addiction is to activity. I'm not referring to the go-getter who gets things done and then takes a vacation. I mean the go-getter who can't stand to stop going and getting. Action is an easy way to keep from being conscious. It can be just as much a way out, an escape from being oneself, as alcohol or morphine or suicide.

If you want to achieve control of any of these addictions, you've first got to see how they come about. They come from the sort of pride that can't admit any kind of dependence, even on God, or perhaps that admits dependence but resents it. They come from the kind of self-centeredness that won't stop looking at the self it doesn't admire. They may come from discontent (which is ingratitude) or boredom (which is sloth), but basically they come from lack of love—lack of real love for God or for oneself.

They come, in short, from plain, old-fashioned sin. Note, please, that I didn't say that the addictions are themselves sins but that they *come from* sin, and every last one of us, addict or not, commits it. The twentieth century has rejected the idea of sin, but its men and women have gone right on sinning. Poor "modern man"! Everybody has told him sin isn't around anymore, so he can do what he likes. He does—and then finds he doesn't like himself. He wants to get out of his own skin and doesn't know how. Not one of the ways he tries will work.

There is only one way it can be done. You can't run away from yourself but you can give yourself away. First you have to give yourself to God. Actually, the people who really do that may not like themselves any better than the addicts do, but it doesn't matter because they have better things than themselves to put their attention on. On God. On His Son, the only man who never sinned at all and yet who shows them how to give themselves away and gives them the power to do it. Finally, on others they can help—you and me, for instance.

16

WRONG GEAR

◈

We keep getting told that this is the age of speed and power. Everything gets put into terms of the automobile, that highly complicated, lethal, automatic symbol of the century. Speed is really the watchword, power comes second.

Most of our automobiles have automatic gears, and they are convenient, but there are times and places where these do us no service. Automatic gears are for smooth going, for level country. In rough country, on steep grades, you need power and you need it direct. Here you have no use for speed.

There is a rough stretch or a steep hill at least somewhere in every life—a stretch where you can't go fast—and you may need more power than you have. All too often we reach these places and find that we have developed habits that act like automatic transmissions. They shift our gears without our having to bother, without our intending, away from the power we need to the speed that can bog us down or that can sometimes be fatal.

Even a highway that looks smooth and level may turn out

to be icy. If we are living by automatic gears, then we have sacrificed dependability for ease. The more we accelerate in a vain hope for power, the more we spin our wheels. We get nowhere, except perhaps in the ditch.

Power for living is available only from God, but that power is not automatic. You have to get it directly or you don't get it at all. You have to be willing to work at living. You have to shift your own gears, ask for and work at accepting the power you need for the life you are living that day. It may come to you through other human beings, through prayer and sacrament, through God's Word or His Church, but you have to do your work in using it.

Some of any man's road is going to be uphill. Some of it will be rough. All of it will be dangerous. Human life in this world is no expressway, and it never will be. To travel it you need power, not speed. The power comes from God, but you must do the driving.

17

WHEN THE
BAND PLAYS

❦

Quincy Quigley is very patriotic. He gets chills up his spine when the band plays "The Stars and Stripes Forever," and he chokes up when the flag goes by.

Amos Adams sometimes feels the same way. He seldom seems to feel that way when he goes to vote. He never feels that way when he pays his taxes.

Mr. Adams is a patriot nonetheless. Maybe he is a patriot even when he criticizes his government, although this is not automatic patriotism either. He was a patriot when he wrote his Congressman (which he has done three times) and when he made a citizen's arrest of a very drunk driver. He didn't feel patriotic at any of these times either. He is usually annoyed when he criticizes the government. He was angry twice when he wrote his Congressman and pleased the third time. He was scared silly when he arrested the drunk. When he votes he is usually bored and occasionally determined. When he pays his taxes—well, you know how he feels when he pays his taxes.

Mr. Adams didn't feel patriotic when he was Corporal Adams either. He didn't even feel like a hero the time they said he was one. Mostly what he felt then, as nearly as he could remember afterwards, was tired.

Mr. Quigley pays his taxes, too, of course. He has to or he would be in trouble. However, he doesn't *quite* pay his taxes. There have been a couple of padded expense reports, and there was the trailer he sold his brother for almost twice what he paid for it. The discrepancy never amounts to more than a few dollars. The government won't miss them; it deals in billions.

Mr. Quigley votes, too. At least sometimes he does. He does when he's got his emotions involved in an election and it isn't raining. The rest of the time? Well, if he really doesn't know much about the candidates, what difference does it make how he votes? Or if he votes?

For all his thrills and chills when the band plays, Mr. Quigley is no patriot when he drops a Kleenex out the car window, or when he says his youngster is eleven at the movie because, after all, his twelfth birthday was only last month.

There are ways in which religion is a lot like patriotism. It *can* be noble feelings and fervent hymn-singing; it can be being inspired or feeling penitent. But religion, like patriotism, is more—a whole lot more—than those feelings. If the feelings are not backed up by some other things, neither the patriotism nor the religion is worth bothering about.

The really religious person is a lot like the really patriotic person. More like Mr. Adams than like Mr. Quigley.

18

TRUTH
AND A NICKEL

❦

You can't see the whole of a nickel. You can see parts of it. You can see two of its three dimensions, but you simply can't see the whole thing. When you look only at one side, you can't see the other one. You can't see the metal inside it; you can't see its atoms and molecules.

A coin is an ordinary thing. Yet a man who can never see the whole of the coin in his pocket may demand to be shown the whole of Truth before he will take any interest in it. Sometimes having seen one side and an edge of the truth about one thing, men think that they have seen all the truth there is.

This has been going on for centuries, for eons. During the Christian Era some men have said that Jesus Christ couldn't possibly be both man and God at the same time. He might be one or the other, but He couldn't be both. They have been talking about God, remember, who is by definition greater than man's imagination can picture and who is Creator of the world those men could never see more than a crumb of, and that only for an instant. Because they couldn't see both sides of God at once, they didn't believe Him.

It still goes on about a lot of things. People can't believe that a church can be both holy and human. They feel they must choose between Word and Sacrament, between Bible and tradition, between faith and work. Men and women try to separate spirit from act, soul from body, love from obedience. People are still saying that God can't (God can't?) be a Holy Trinity and still be the One God because they can't see both sides of the proposition at once.

They still can't see both sides of the coins in their pockets, either, but they believe in *them*.

19

SUPERCARGO

❦

Everybody knows why, at least before more powerful planes were built, there was (and sometimes there still is) a limit to the amount of baggage allowed to be carried by each air passenger. Aircraft engines are designed to carry a certain weight, and to exceed that weight is perilous. Occasionally when it has lost an engine a military plane, for instance, has had to jettison everything in it that was loose except the people in order to lighten its load to what might be safely borne by its remaining power. The reason airplanes are equipped with wing deicers is that ice adds to the weight that engines must keep aloft.

A plane may fly with a full load, or even with a slight overload, as long as its course is "straight and level." If it needs to gain altitude to bypass a storm or miss a mountain, if there is engine failure, then excess baggage has to go.

Most of us carry a lot of excess baggage through life: bundles and bags that weigh us down, cartons and crates of frozen attitudes and fossilized emotions that overload us. As long as our course is straight and level, these things don't seem to matter, but when we get off course and find a mountain looming up in front of us, or when towering cumulus brews ahead, then these things have to be jettisoned. To hang onto them is to risk catastrophe. The choice may be between these things and life itself.

What is this excess baggage in our hearts and souls? What are the things we transport through life at the risk of disaster?

The armaments of hate are probably the heaviest. Even one hate weighs much, and the longer you carry it, the greater its load.

The smaller weapons of personal prejudice are heavy, too, because they are the handguns of hate that we carry every day without even knowing that we have them. But we use them, unthinkingly, and they can kill.

The rags of ignorance and the dirt of sloth weigh more than you would think to look at them. The iron of ambition adds to the load; so does the unmelting dry ice of fear. The tightly sealed sack of self-centeredness, all by itself, weighs more than our baggage allowance amounts to.

We all really know that storms may require that these things be jettisoned, but when we hit rough weather, it may already be too late. We may find that we cannot tear them loose from their storage places. After all, if we have had them stowed there for a long time, they may be wedged in immovably. If they are stuck, we are stuck with them. Even if we do have time to pry them loose, we will likely need help in doing it, and in rough going everybody has his own work to do. The time to loosen our excess baggage, the time to get help if we need it, the time to throw these things out is now, while our course is straight and level.

Already the horizon is a little hazy and bears watching.

20

TRANSLATION

❧

Whenever you translate from one language into another, you find that you have to take liberties with words in order to preserve the sense. A precisely literal translation of any statement is an impossibility, but even if it were possible, such a translation would still lose meaning in one way or another.

Whenever you translate, not from one language into another but from spiritual terms into physical, from the eternal to the temporal, you have the same problem many times magnified. The difficulty is infinitely worse than that of translating, say, French into English or Russian into Spanish. It is more like translating from a highly sophisticated and subtle tongue into a primitive one without written characters and with a limited vocabulary. You lose quality, descriptive power, accuracy, and force in the process. If you are familiar with the original in such a language and read the translation, you keep feeling, "But that's not really what it said. That's hardly even the barest bones of it."

This is the real problem of Bible translation. I don't

mean the fact that the King James Version with all its majesty and power to inspire is a translation of a translation of a translation, nor the fact that the deliberately modern translations because they are up to date will sound extremely old-fashioned in a few years. The difficulties of these situations are obvious. The real problem of the Bible is not that our version is a translation of Greek and Hebrew into some other language but that the Bible itself is a translation of the eternal into the temporal.

It was this sticky point that led scholars to come up with the term "myth," and no greater disservice has ever been done to any sacred scripture. Scholars used the word in a theologically technical sense, but to any ordinary man "myth" means something very different from what they intended. Myth, as the word is commonly used, is exactly the opposite of what the Christian Bible contains. Myth, outside the technical meaning, is a fictional explanation of natural phenomena.

Our Bible is the record of spiritual phenomena, and it isn't meant to be an explanation of anything. There are plenty of religious explanations around, but you don't find them in the Bible. The miracles recorded in the Bible are not somebody's way of explaining natural events. Just the reverse: They are the reporting of unnatural events that couldn't be accounted for. If somebody tells you such stories can't be true because water doesn't usually turn into wine and dead men don't customarily walk around alive again, they're not only stating the obvious, they are woefully missing the point. If water were likely to turn into wine and if men habitually rose from the dead in this world, nobody would have thought it remarkable enough to mention it in the first place. The Bible is not a report of what might have been expected, it is a report of the utterly unexpected.

This library of books we call the Bible is written about ordinary men and women all right, but its reason for being is that it is written about the extraordinary things God has done and does with them. It doesn't matter in the least how many days Genesis says were spent in the creation of the world; the point it makes and makes in its first sentence is that the world was made by God. Disagree with the Bible's physics or geography or mathematics because it simply isn't concerned with physics and geography and mathematics. It is the true story of God's dealing with men. On this subject it is infallible.

The Bible does present these subjects in translation, not so much from language to language as from sphere to sphere, and we have to remember what that means—that this is a translation from the highly complex to the utterly elementary, from the artistic to the crude, in short, from the eternal to the temporal. In this process some things must be left out, but nothing is added. The result of such translation is not a stretching of the truth; it is always less than the truth. The Bible's hints of the glory, the majesty, the infinite holiness of God, are but the merest clues to their reality. The Bible's accounts of the shattering miracles of His working in the souls of men and women don't come anywhere near to the seemingly incredible truth. Spiritual reality is always infinitely greater than the way the Bible shows it to us, which is undoubtedly just as well. If we have trouble in grasping the translation into what might be called Basic Human, how should we be able to bear the impact of the original?

The resurrection of the slain Son of God was nothing *less* than His recorded appearance to His followers—but it was also much more than that. The Incarnation was nothing less than His virgin conception but it was also far beyond that. The coming of the Holy Ghost was not mere flame and storm and compelling rhetoric in each hearer's native tongue. It was that, but it was also more.

Read the Bible for what it is, a translation. Only so will you prepare to learn someday the original language and to know eternally the awesome fullness of the meaning to which our Bible can but barely introduce us, here and now.

21

THE PARISH
BAKE SHOP

In a midwestern village there is a little shop on the square that bears a sign over the door: "Bake Shop." Inside you can find cigarettes, candy, a cup of coffee, magazines, comic books, and pinball machines. No bread.

There are parish churches like that. The sign of Christ is on them saying that they offer nourishment to the starving, but inside you find only diversion, stimulation, entertainment, social (in one meaning) activity or social (in another sense) action. But not bread.

It is not only the cross on the steeple or the cornerstone that proclaims to the neighborhood that a church offers food for the spirits of men; everything about it that says "church" does the same. Whatever, by custom or association, designates a church as Christian advertises to men that it can nourish and strengthen them with the Bread of the World.

Sometimes what men find inside is only candy; sweet promises of emotional ease and optimism, the lulling, lying news that they are good and have nothing in themselves to fear, instead of the Good News that they are sinners to whom God offers over and over the bread that is salvation and eternal life. Sometimes men find stimulants in their churches, things designed to keep them so keyed up and busy that they are left with neither time, energy, nor awareness even to perceive their own real hunger, much less the basic spiritual hunger of others.

If men are offered bread and then refused it, they are cheated no matter what else they are given, no matter what else they may even think that they want. The cross is the sign that real, life-giving bread has been broken and offered to the world, that any man may eat it and be forever satisfied. Only a church can provide that bread. Any substitution offered for it is a cheat.

22

HUMAN ALGEBRA

❧

When I studied algebra in high school (long, long before the new math), we did equations—what seemed like millions of equations. We were always trying to find out what x represented. Our old friend x, of course, was the unknown quantity.

Every now and then in the course of our adult lives we come up against things that don't work out the way common sense or experience, or the computers, say they should. A juvenile delinquent grows up into a prominent scientist; a no-good drunk becomes the most responsible man in town; a shotgun wedding turns into a marriage; a dying man outlives his doctors; an utterly self-centered woman turns into a delightful saint. These things don't happen very often but they happen. I have seen them. When they do, the equation has our old friend x in it—the unknown quantity. The figures we can see, no matter how we arrange them, could never produce such results.

Still it isn't really the unknown quantity that accounts for this, it is more an unknown quality. It is X, upper case, instead of x, lower case. (Is it mere circumstance that the capital X has for centuries been a symbol for Christ, and that when we write "Xmas" for "Christmas" we are being in no way flippant?)

X, in such cases, must stand for the power of God. When that power is absent from the human equation, the answers are distressingly predictable; when that power enters you can't predict the answers at all. With monotonous regularity things turn out for people in just the way that the social scientists and statisticians say they will, but wherever somebody has brought in X, all bets are off. In this new kind of equation the result can be almost anything.

Some of these results are so momentous, so exciting, that they make it pretty ridiculous for anyone, ever, to think of Christianity as dull. How can it be dull when you not only don't know what you might be doing, you don't even know what kind of a person you may be tomorrow or next year, or fifteen hundred years from now? How can it be dull when the power of X is so great that you can spend the rest of your life finding out about what X represents—and never come to the end of it?

It is the statistically monotonous human equation without X that is dull. It's the presence of X that can make life a never-ending wonder.

23

THERE'S A
WAR ON

❦

You can't send raw recruits into battle, or at least you had better not. Untrained civilians not only would last no longer under fire than an ice cube in the oven, they would serve no purpose. If you've got a war on, you'd better fight it with trained men and functioning equipment.

Militarily this is axiomatic. It ought to be axiomatic in the spiritual area as well. The real enemies of Christianity—and of every Christian—are real, many, and formidable, for all that you can't see them. Again and again churches—and the individual Christians—send against them no more than a den of Cub Scouts armed with cap pistols. What can the result be but defeat?

A defeated congregation may look victorious to the neighborhood. After all, it may look just *like* the neighborhood. But in actuality, it may be in spiritual rout from the field, just as a "pillar of the church" may be spiritually licked. Whether a congregation's defeat takes the form of internal dissension, complacency, inertia, scandal, apostasy, or dissolution, a large part of the reason for its downfall is that its members are untrained, undisciplined. When a war starts it is already too late to start drafting men. By then the time for close-order drill and the manual of arms is long past.

When crises come along it is also too late for the individual Christian to start marshaling his resources. There has always been a war on for him. He enlisted when he was baptized, and he can't wait until a battle begins in his front yard to start learning his left foot from his right one.

It is surprisingly difficult to learn how to pray; developing self-discipline is never easy. It is impossible to acquire a Christian sense of values—after the shooting begins. The shooting itself is too distracting and, of course, too deadly. Every church ought to offer a good solid course in complete recruit-training for Christians. Does yours?

What kind of a soldier are you? Disciplined? Trained? Equipped? Do you know the enemy and his methods? Do you know where the front lines are? Do you even know your own weapons?

24

WHAT GOD?

❦

There is an ancient saying that men become like that which they worship. It does seem to work out that way.

People who worship gold, those to whom wealth is worth sacrifice, generally become hard. People who worship pleasure, people to whom pleasure is the greatest thing there is, tend to become soft, even flabby. People who worship fame, people who give their lives to the pursuit of acclaim, become shallow. People who worship power, people who can honor only might, tend to become tyrants.

People who worship only themselves—oh, but all of these people worship themselves in the end. The gods they bow to are really the gods they hope to climb above. The gods to whom they give themselves are the gods they hope somehow to possess.

To worship gold is to want to acquire it, to be greater even than gold. To worship pleasure is to desire to be master of pleasure. To worship fame is to desire glory. To worship power is to seek the means of ruling.

Now, what you worship is not only what you honor, what you kneel to. It is what you rely on, what you trust in, what you love. Worship is sacrifice, and what you would give the most for is what you really adore. Do you trust in wealth to save you from the uncertainties of life? Do you give up character and honor in exchange for pleasure? Do you rely on the power of your status or position? Do you spend your life in the hope of achieving fame?

Christians who really do worship the God they claim to worship, the God revealed in Jesus Christ, tend to become like Jesus. The process is gradual, piecemeal, but their neighbors or the people who work with them, or their clients or patients or bosses, can at least catch glimpses that reflect the God these people love, though they themselves are unaware of it. Such Christians trust in God, not in anything the world can furnish. They would rather achieve character than status. They would rather be wholly human than just happy. The only people they want to rule are themselves.

Whom do you worship? Well, what are you like? Better yet, what do your neighbors think you are like?

25

THE SICK MAN

❧

Mr. X didn't feel very good. As time went on, he kept feeling worse, and Mrs. X told him he ought to go see a doctor. Mr. X didn't really want to go to a doctor, so he tried to figure out what was wrong all by himself. He tried old prescriptions in the medicine cabinet and almost everything advertised at the drug store.

Finally Mr. X could hardly get out of bed in the morning, so he consented to see a doctor, but he had read an ad about a kind of doctor who could cure anything in no time at all, so he went to see him. Then Mr. X had to go back to see him some more, and he had to pay him a good deal of money, but he still didn't feel one bit better than he had when he was trying to cure himself. If anything, he felt worse.

At last Mr. X took his wife's advice and went to their family doctor—the man they always called when the children were sick. There aren't many such physicians around nowadays, but there are some and it begins to look as if there may be more again. This doctor examined Mr. X, listened to him, gave him some medicine to take, and told him he must lose weight. He gave Mr. X a diet to follow.

Two months later Mr. X sadly told his wife that he guessed there just wasn't any cure for him since he was still sick. He thought perhaps he was going to die, and he felt very sorry for himself. But Mrs. X didn't seem to feel very sorry for him because all she said was, "Well, I know you haven't taken that medicine, because the bottle is still almost full. You certainly haven't taken off any weight." Mr. X sounds awfully familiar to most of us. We know somebody just like him. It may be that it is we who sound just like him, and what is wrong includes our lives instead of just our bodies.

We know something is wrong because we feel terrible. We're depressed, or anxious, or we feel guilty or ashamed. We don't have the ambition, the plans, or the hope we used to have for the future, and the present seems to be just something to get lived through somehow.

We try to figure out what's the matter; we try to think of something to do about it. We try first one thing and then another, and none of it works.

We finally give up and admit we need help, and we go looking for it. Where? Why, to the neighbors, or to books and magazine articles, or to some self-constituted expert who claims to have all the answers.

Then we wind up worse off than ever. We decide we've really had it, that there's no help for what we've got. We think our difficulty must be something new, something rare, undoubtedly something fatal. But it probably isn't new or rare at all, though it may prove fatal if we procrastinate long enough. It is probably as common and as old a thing as sin. In fact, it may well *be* sin.

Maybe we finally consent to try God. We go to church. We listen to sermons. We even read the Bible. Somewhere in all this we get a diagnosis (oh yes, we do—we may pretend we don't hear it, but we get told). We get a prescription, and we find out what we have to do.

The medicine doesn't taste very good. What we have to do is a nuisance, a worry.

We say that we don't have a good doctor and we feel very sorry for ourselves.

26

NO DEADHEADS

Back when railroads carried passengers, one of them issued a pass to a physician who lived in the town that was the railroad's section point. The doctor worked for that pass, treating workmen at all hours of the day and night.

One day his wife boarded the train and presented the pass to the conductor. "Sorry, lady," said the conductor. "This railroad doesn't issue any *family* passes."

An attorney was playing golf with friends one Sunday morning. "I went to church early," one man said. "Oh, I let my wife go to church for the family," said the lawyer.

"Oh, I'm terribly busy," said a young woman who had been asked to visit a nursing home inmate. "Mother does so much of that sort of thing. I don't have time."

On the road to joy, here or hereafter, there are no family passes.

27

PERFECT
UNDERSTANDING

略

HE: My wife doesn't really understand me.

SHE: Maybe she does understand you better than you like.

For all our adolescent tears at being misunderstood—and our later ones, too, for that matter—being understood is no unmixed blessing. It's rather belittling. It means the other person is smarter than we took him to be, maybe smarter than we are. It means he's bigger than we are and more mature.

Being understood means, too, that we're not as complex as we thought ourselves, not as interesting, not as different from everybody else. It means we're not as clever as we thought we were. If somebody understands us, they have our number, they're on to us. Our poses begin to look silly, if we're understood. Our gestures get a little limp.

This is one reason not everybody likes to go to church. Not everybody wants even to think about a God who can understand him, much less to come in contact with such a God. You can have all kinds of different ideas about God, but if He is God at all, then he understands human beings. He understands you. To have God understand you is no more comfortable, no more ego-supporting, no more flattering than it is to have your husband or your mother or your boss or your teacher understand you.

Of course, He is God and He's *supposed* to be wiser, bigger, mightier than we are. Still, there is the little thought that He understands us all the way. Every little bit. Nothing hidden. Nothing at all? That's an uncomfortable thought. Makes you feel kind of silly, doesn't it?

Maybe I'd rather just be misunderstood. Maybe I can find somebody I can impress. . . . Being understood, especially by God, is costly.

28

LAMPS

❦

I know a store in which there is nothing but lamps—thousands of lamps. Some are modern, some are antique, some are ornate, some plainly utilitarian. Some of them are plugged into sockets and turned on.

One day a little girl in that store said to her mother, "I like the ones best where the light shines out."

Christianity is, you might say, full of churches—millions of churches. Some are starkly or richly modern, some are Gothic or Romanesque or Georgian. Some are richly ornamented with stained glass and carved wood; some have plywood furniture and folding chairs.

Some few of these churches win prizes from architectural committees, while others are known as eyesores and monstrosities to the artistically sensitive. God, I think, likes best the ones where the light shines out.

The real beauty of a church, like the real beauty of a bulldozer, lies in how well it serves the end for which it was built. It is all well and good, when building a church, to make it as attractive as you can to passers-by, and this is really more important than making it significant to a committee of experts who will seldom come near it. But the first requirement in a church is the same as the first requirement in a lamp. How well does it light things up?

The light that shines from a church has nothing to do with its windows or its electrical system. It has to do with the holiness of the people who live in it and the revealing illumination cast by the things they believe in. The church that lights the neighborhood is the church whose people shed warmth and glory there and, also important, whose teachings set a standard of wholeness and health of spirit and mind. The church that lights up a city is the church whose people truly believe in the one, holy God, and whose lives reflect, as they can, His holiness—not just ethics or friendliness—in that city. A city can get its ethics from a lot of other sources and friendliness from even more, so while these things are important, it is not really up to the churches to supply them. Churches are the only places where holiness can shine.

You may know what the architects think about your church and you may or may not agree with them. If you want to know how much light it sheds, find out what kind of difference its people and the things they honestly believe in make in their offices, in their spacious or crowded neighborhoods, in their schools and hospitals and organizations, in their homes.

Better still, see what kind of a difference *you* make. Is any place lighted up by your presence? Is there anywhere that is brighter and better when you are there?

29

WHO'S BEHIND
THE WHEEL?

❦

The atmosphere of today is compounded of a sense of speed, a sense of helplessness, and a sense of frustration, heavily tinged with fear and bewilderment.

It is a lot like the six-year-old who climbed in the car and managed to get it started. Being very sure that he could drive it if he had the chance, he careened down the street, frantically twisting the steering wheel and kicking first one pedal and then another.

At first he liked it. It was exciting. Then he became a little bit nervous. Then he got mad. Then he began to be scared. Finally, he was terrified and he sobbed, "Daddy, daddy," as the car smashed into a tree.

The young man who gets behind the wheel of his life and takes it out on his own is excited at first. That's why he usually tries so hard to look blasé. When a few things go wrong, he begins to get a bit nervous. When he starts to feel that the car is running away with him, he gets frightened. He may cry for Daddy like the six-year-old, although he does it his own way. The trouble with both the child and the young man is that it wasn't Daddy who neglected them; it was they who ran away from Daddy—away from rules, authority, above all, from letting someone else drive the car.

The Christian (when he is acting like a Christian) lets his Father drive his life. He can enjoy some of the trip, and even when the road is rough or frightening he still knows that he is really safe. He may not know exactly where he is going, but he knows he will arrive where he wants to be, because the driving isn't up to him.

30

NEED GLASSES?

❧§ৡ❧

People used to buy their spectacles in stores, the same way they bought chewing gum or a loaf of bread, but this seldom proved a satisfactory way to aid failing eyesight. The reason is that eyes fail in different ways. It takes learning and skill to find out what is wrong with a man's eyes and to prescribe the lens that will correct the trouble.

There is nearsightedness. The nearsighted person lives in a small world. Until he gets his glasses he may never see the top of a tree. He doesn't know his friends until he is close enough to touch them. Nearsightedness can be dangerous. You can't see peril coming. You can't help when you are needed. Getting around at all is a strain.

There is farsightedness. The farsighted person is always unsure of what is nearest to him. Because he can't read comfortably, he may have a hard time learning a lot of things.

There is astigmatism. This is sight that twists things out of shape. Your eyes may distort the things you see, whether they are nearsighted or farsighted, or neither.

The same things can go wrong with men's vision as go wrong with their sight. Failing vision is even more dangerous than failing sight because vision is so much more important to living than sight. The way you see life may be near-sighted or it may be farsighted, or you may just see life crooked.

Nearsighted vision is the most common and most of us suffer from it to some degree. We can't see anything clearly until it affects us personally. The only thing that is real to us is ourselves. We are the center of a small, small world. We can't tell our friends from our enemies; we can't see the woods for the trees; we can't see danger ahead. We can't help anybody who needs us, because we are unaware of the need. Life is narrow to those whose vision is so constricted, and living is a strain.

Some, however, suffer from farsighted vision. They are kind to strangers while they mistreat or ignore their families. They plan great things for the future but they waste today. They know the basic principles of a good life but they can't seem to put those principles into practice. They can see other people's faults but not their own.

Living with this kind of faulty vision is dangerous too. You are always tripping on the little things under your feet. You don't see the need that is right around you. You don't see the help that is near you either. It's hard to learn.

Then there's astigmatic vision. Either the farsighted or the nearsighted can have this. The man whose vision is otherwise perfect may have it. His vision warps what he looks at. He sees wholesome things as evil. He sees evil things as good.

He sees the temporary as permanently important and the enduring as insignificant. He is in a far worse state than the merely nearsighted or farsighted man because he can't think straight, and, worse, he can't even love straight. Because he can't tell good from evil, he can't tell help from danger, and his end is disaster. If he is a leader, many others share that disaster.

There are a lot of oculists to whom you can go for the correction of your faulty sight, but only God can correct your faulty vision. He will do so, if you let Him—but first you have to admit that you need glasses.

31

SYMBOLS

❧

Every so often somebody blasts some part of Christianity for being, or using, "mere symbolism." I doubt that there exists such a thing as a "mere" symbol, and the U.S. government seems to agree.

The Federal Trade Commission once forbade two perfume distributors from continuing to use French names and *symbols* on perfume that was produced in the United States. Understand, there were no statements involved in this misleading packaging, only fleur de lis and the Eiffel Tower, but the FTC apparently thought symbols could lie as effectively as words.

Never underestimate the power of a symbol. It can take money out of a pocket and it can put courage into a heart. It can win votes and influence legislation. It can start a revolution.

To say that a thing is a symbol is not to say that that is all it is. A house may be a symbol of the family who lives there, or a symbol of success, or a symbol of a new architectural era. It could be all these symbols at once. It could still be a home. A home is a great deal more than a symbol; but it is always a symbol, too.

You can't ignore a thing because it is just a symbol, because symbols may be powerful. A thing may be a symbol and a great deal else besides. It may even be a symbol that is true.

The symbols on the perfume packages were not true. They lied about the contents of the packages. It wasn't the use of symbols to which the Federal Trade Commission objected. It was the fact that the symbols were designed to mislead.

The symbols on the Christian package, however, are true. They don't mislead people; they lead them to grace and glory and the knowledge of the love of God. The Cross is the symbol of the victory of the Son of God over our sin and our death, and millions of Christians have known that victory for themselves.

32

WHO IS STRONG?

ఞఢఞ

Wallace never got tired of showing Tom how strong he was. "See that big rock over there?" he asked. "I'll bet I can split it in three blows with this pick." He didn't succeed in three blows. After twelve tries he got tired and quit. Then Tom felt a little better. He was so sick of hearing how strong his cousin was. Before they left the big boulder Tom picked a seed out of a pine cone and dropped it into a little depression in the rock and covered it over with a handful of dirt. Thirty years later, if he had remembered, Tom could have said to Wallace, "I was stronger than you were. I split the rock without any blows at all. It took time, not force." The roots of a pine tree did what the pick could not.

This world we live in is always bragging about how strong it is. Force, the world keeps telling us, can break anything it sets out to break.

You'd think the world would have learned by now that the little weak things of the earth can sometimes burst apart the strongest defenses of the mighty. Seemingly unimportant events manage to topple thrones. Tiny mosquitos and tinier microbes defeat the armies of empires. Little drops of rainwater level mountains. Little people change the course of history. Little habits undermine great characters.

Little prayers and acts of love let God act in us in great and wonderful ways so that, little by little, we find joy while the big strong world around us goes looking vainly for happiness.

33

POINT OF VIEW

❧

Take a stained-glass window. Walk by a church someday and look at one in a good light. It isn't very impressive. *Stained* glass? There is hardly any color in it at all. Glass? It might just about as well be boiler plate.

Somebody paid a lot of perfectly good money to have that window put in that building and they must have had a reason. No matter how hard you look from outside, you can't imagine what the reason could have been.

Well, go on. Go inside. You might get involved, but that involvement was worth a lot to somebody. Aren't you curious to know why?

Yes, it is the same window. You didn't get your directions mixed. It is the being inside versus outside that makes all that difference.

Of course it is stained glass. Where else can you find that glowing color, that depth and intensity of light? The day that shines through that window doesn't look like the ordinary daylight you had seen outside.

The faith of Christians is like that window. If it seems dark, dull, or dismal you are looking at it from the wrong direction. You can't see very much from the doorway of Christianity either, but people who go all the way inside find it worth spending their lives for. They find it to be the source of beauty and of light.

Go on in, *all the way in*, and take a look. And see glory.

34

GETTING READY

When a man plans to go fishing he may spend most of the night before getting ready for the trip. He checks his tackle. Then he packs—everything he might conceivably need the next day, plus a few things that can't possibly be necessary.

When a woman prepares for a weekend visit, she considers what she might do on that visit and then packs everything she could conceivably need for any eventuality: cosmetics packed so they won't spill, dresses packed so they won't wrinkle, all the jewelry she might want and all the accessories she might need. And some things she won't possibly use.

What happens when most Christians go to church? Sure, their hats may be on and their shoes shined, but there will most likely be a last-minute rush for the pledge money. Then they are off with barely time to make it before the service begins.

Clothes were the last thing the fisherman bothered about. His real care, time, and effort went into seeing that the tackle was sufficient and in order. Maybe he got out in the back yard and flipped a fly around a bit to get his hand in again.

The woman was concerned about clothes but not about what she would wear on the way. She anticipated the entertainment that would be provided and made sure she would be suitably dressed for that.

If the fisherman got to the stream without flies, his trip would be wasted. If the woman hadn't the right clothes for the party, she would hate every moment of it.

Yet they both wonder why they don't get much satisfaction out of going to church. They know they have done a duty when they go, but they have a sneaking feeling that there ought to be more to it than that. Maybe they enjoy the music, but if that is all, the morning will still seem unfinished. And it will be.

They are right. There ought to be more to it because there *is* more to it—a lot more. It feels unfinished because it is—for them. The worship of God on Sunday was never intended to be a break in a God-ignoring week. Christian worship was never meant to be a thing thoughtlessly turned on for an hour and turned off without recall. It must be prepared for beforehand and used afterward.

If the fisherman prepared for church as he prepares to go fishing, he would go over his prayers and his praises, try his use of them, and limber up his figurative knees. The woman would think of the house she was going to and the Host who had invited her and go prepared to fit into what was to go on. She would take the humility and trustfulness, the

87

penitence and receptiveness that are the proper garments to wear in the house of God.

The time for preparing for church is not the last few moments before you drive off on Sunday morning. The time is all the week before. The prayers you say on Monday and Wednesday are your preparation for Sunday and so is helping your neighbor on Tuesday. If you should hurt someone on Friday, repentance for that must go with you to church and so must your asking what to do about it.

A church service doesn't begin when the choir sings an opening hymn. It begins when the choir sings the closing one on the previous Sunday. The rest of the week you get your tackle ready and you think what you will wear (spiritually).

When you prepare before you go to church, you will find that there will be more to it than you ever knew there was.

35
FROM MISSOURI

Who hasn't gotten himself a painful sunburn on a cloudy day? The light may have been dull and the sky overcast so you stayed out fishing or swimming; by the next day you had a burn that you still remember. You couldn't see the sun, but the sun was there, and potent.

It's the ultraviolet light that does the dirty work of course. That is the light that your eyes can't even see as light. When clouds screen out the visible light, you may forget that the ultraviolet is still coming through—and can still burn.

Have you ever tried one of those whistles that are used to call dogs home without bothering neighbors? When you blow one of those whistles, you can't hear them but the dogs do. Their sound is audible to canine ears but not to human ones.

The next time you hear someone pooh-pooh the power of God in human affairs or the next time you feel inclined to laugh off the effects of prayer, think again. Remember the sunburn and the whistle.

It is not that God is like the sun, even though a lot of civilizations have thought that the sun was a god. It is not that prayer is at all like a whistle that God will come to when no one else can hear it. Still, these things can be a reminder that, even when we have looked with our eyes and listened with our ears, the evidence is not all in. If we won't believe what we can't see, we may get burned. You might say that there are sounds that we can't hear that someone else can.

"Show me," is really a pretty poor test for anything. The con man can always manage to pass that test; the angels may not bother. The stage magician and the shell game artist can make you see what isn't there at all. What *is* there may be something you have to see with a different kind of vision. The voices that the prophets and St. Joan of Arc heard are not the kind of sound that you can hear just by turning off the television. You have to have the right kind of ears and be used to using them.

Of course there are a lot of things in this life that have to be proved by sight and by sound, by figures and experiments and measures and scales. You don't become a saint by accepting that kind of thing without its own kind of proof, you just become gullible. But you can't prove love that way. You can't prove God that way.

If you are going to look for the "show me" kind of proof for everything, you are going to make just as much of a mess of your life as the man who risks his fortune on a gamble. In fact, you will make a worse mess. All he loses is his money. You can lose your life—your real and eternal life.

Christianity has been teaching people for over two thousand years how to know the presence of the invisible, how to hear the sounds of the inaudible, how to live and live joyously in the whole total life that Jesus Christ brought to men, no matter how grim the visible world may look or how bad the news you hear with your ears.

36

THE SIMPLE
GOSPEL

❧❧❧

Every Christian teacher from St. Paul on has been accused
of complicating the simple Gospel of Jesus Christ. The Gospel itself, said a man I know, is as simple as branch water.

All right. Have a look at branch water—the fluid that
makes up what the poets once would have called a brook.
Sometimes it is a liquid, sometimes a solid, sometimes a gas.
It is made up of the combined molecules of two elements,
those molecules being made up of moving protons and elec-
trons arranging themselves in what is hardly a simple pattern
by anybody's definition. It is not a rigid pattern, either, and
it is constantly in motion. It is more like a dance than anything else.

Then there is the material that gets added to the branch
water and becomes a part of it. From the soil around it and
from the air above it and in it come organic materials, in-
organic materials, microscopic life in animal and vegetable
and as yet indistinguishable kinds, submicroscopic life, visible
life, fishes and crustaceans and snakes and animals and birds

plus all the by-products of their life in the stream. And there's man, too. He is a part of the world of the stream, and branch water is hardly anywhere now devoid of his chemicals, fertilizers, pesticides, and detergents, among other things.

Then there are all the things that branch water does. It rises in the stream and floods the soil, eroding it. It goes through systems of canals to irrigate crops. It furnishes hydroelectric power. It goes through purification systems that take out some of its chemicals and add others. It furnishes the means of hydrotherapy by which human ailments of mind and body are treated. It gets things clean; it gets things dirty.

Branch water becomes vapor and rises to great heights in the sky. It falls as rain. It freezes and falls as hail and snow. Snow drifts, packs, and becomes ice.

The branch runs into the river and the river into the sea. There the simple branch water . . . want to go on? That is only the beginning.

The Good News of God's restoration of man to His love may very well be as simple as the branch water He made. But it is not one patterned snowflake simpler.

37

A LEAF
AND ELISHA

❧

I remember that when I was very young I found it interesting that I could, in a sense, command the sun to go away and then to come back again. The process was simple: When I was lying on the grass under a tree, a slight move of my head could put a leaf between my eye and the sun and make the sun, for me, disappear. Another slight move and the sun was back again, shining into my eye until I shut it.

There was a heady little feel to this process in the trivial way of a summer afternoon. I felt just a little bit like Elisha commanding the sun, although the similarity didn't occur to me then because I had never heard of Elisha. Shutting my eyes tight might keep the sun out of them, but this was not the same. Shutting your eyes admitted that the sun was there; indeed, it was a surrender to the sun. Blotting the sun out with a leaf was a kind of victory.

A lot of adults use the same process to blot out God. These are neither the atheists nor the blatant libertines. Both the self-announced atheist and the self-advertised sinner are shutting their eyes tight to keep God out, admitting God's power, really, by the force of their denial. The people who blot God out are those who so easily (just a slight movement of the head will do it) put a leaf between themselves and the sun.

A leaf is a fragile thing and lasts at most but a season. The sun is mighty, and today's sunlight burned how long ago? The leaves by which we blot out God are fragile things, too, and short-lived: status, money, things, power, revenge, yesterday's disappointments, and tomorrow's desires. All these things and more are merely the leaves of summer. Yet we can permit, or even force, those leaves to come between us and God, the sun without which we could not even exist.

Move your head a little. See what you may be blotting out of your life.

38

THE EMPTY PEW

❧§❧

Her church meant a lot in the life of Mrs. Burch, and the time finally came when she looked down the pew she sat in and felt quietly thankful. There was the whole Burch family together in church, just as she had so long dreamed that they might one day be. Mr. Burch had started coming back to church again after many years of neglect, and the children were old enough to know what was going on and to take part in it. Now she had a further mental picture of the Burch family pew as the children grew up and the parents got older. It was a pretty picture, and she prayed that it would be that way.

It wasn't that way. A few years later she suddenly realized that she was in the pew alone again, just as she had been when she was first married. Yet the family members were all in church. Andrew was in church in another city, where he was in school. Tom and Sue were in the choir. Jane was teaching Sunday School. Mr. Burch was an usher.

"How funny," thought Mrs. Burch. "I really didn't get what I asked for. Then again, I did—only I got a lot more of it than I ever could have imagined."

Planning your future? Planning the future for those you love? Maybe God has even better things in mind than you do.

39

EYE ON THE TARGET

❦

If you're going to become a marksman, you have to learn three basic rules about shooting firearms. The first rule is that you have to keep your eye on the target. You can never hit anything (that you want to hit, that is) by looking at the end of the gun. The second rule is that you must squeeze the trigger slowly and evenly. You must not, absolutely not, pull it with a jerk. The third rule is that you have to go out to the target range and use up a lot of ammunition practicing.

These rules are not unrelated to some rules of the spiritual life. If you are going to try to be a really functioning Christian, you will have to remember three things.

The first is to keep your eye on the target. You can't keep looking at yourself to see how you're doing. Indeed, you can't keep your eye on yourself and come anywhere near what you are aiming at. A lot of Christians think that you can become like Jesus Christ by watching your step. What you really need to do is watch Him. You become like people by looking at them, not your own mirror. All you do if you keep an eye on yourself is either start admiring how good you are or despairing at how bad you are—and both are way off target.

The second thing to remember is that you can't become a Christian saint (which is to say an effective disciple of our Lord) instantaneously. Only the exertion of a slow, steady, unwavering strength keeps your aim true while you are firing, so don't panic, don't rush. Impatience never yet hit a proper target, material or spiritual. Those who jerk the trigger make a lot of noise, but their shots go wild. Steady and persevering is the right pace.

The third thing to remember is that it does you no good at all to memorize the first two rules, or any other rules, if you don't get out on the range and keep firing, putting them into practice. Ammunition in the box doesn't make you a marksman. You have to spend your ammunition, spend yourself, over and over and over, and then begin again.

The same three basic principles apply to firing a gun or living your religion: Keep your eye on the target, keep steady, keep trying.

40

COUNTERFEITS

Every once in a while you learn that a lot of counterfeit money has gotten into circulation. Somebody has made clever copies of the stuff we use to get food and clothes and fun, the stuff we exchange for what we want and need. To the casual observer counterfeit money looks just like real money. It has to or it would not get into wallets and banks. It is shaped the same; it is the same color; the words and symbols on it are just the same. Yet it is worthless. The difference is not in the money itself, it is in what is behind that money. Counterfeit bills are paper, and that is all they are. Real ones are assurances that a government stands behind their assertion of value.

A lot of other things get counterfeited too. People may wind up with a pocket full of worthless bills that look just like the real things but are not worth the space they take up. These people think that they have acquired something of value; they think that they are rich. When they try to use their phoney money, they discover that they are broke.

Joy is probably one of the most counterfeited riches in the world. Counterfeits of that are so common that few people know what the real thing is. Pleasure may look just like joy, and a lot of people think that is what it is. But not even happiness is the real thing.

Love gets counterfeited as often as joy. Love has a lot of different counterfeits. Romance is one. Sex is one. Friendship is one and so is pity. Affection, admiration, even curiosity, can be counterfeits of love. They all feel a lot like love when you handle them.

Christianity gets counterfeited a lot also. High ideals, respectability, good nature, and sentiment can be imitations of the real thing. So can self-righteousness, fear, habit, and convention. So can superstition. Any of these can look a lot like Christianity, and some of them even get marked with the right words.

The counterfeits can be so much like the real thing, but the problem is that there is never anything standing behind these counterfeits to guarantee their worth, never anything backing them up, nothing to give them meaning and substance. The counterfeits will not stand up under pressure. They crumble, they tear, they dissolve. When things get hot, they melt. They wear thin very quickly. In truth they just aren't real—they are phoney.

Do you think you are rich? Take a good close look at your wealth. If you're hoarding counterfeits, that future you count on could be pretty blank.

But if you can obtain even a little bit of real honest-to-God (and the phrase is not meant casually) Christianity, love, and joy, then your future is bright indeed. Then it is not only your future that is truly secure and bright. Even your present is rich beyond measure.

41

CRUTCHES IN
THE CHAPEL

❧

Long ago I knew a little chapel in New Orleans where all around the altar hung crutches, plaster casts from broken arms and legs, and a lot of other things that looked more as if they belonged in a hospital trash can than in a house of worship. There is many a place in the world where such a scheme of decoration prevails in a sanctuary.

Esthetically, such things are shocking; evangelically, they may be a detriment; liturgically, they are undoubtedly a nuisance. Yet there is reason in them and there is a lesson in them, particularly for those of us who worship in neat conventional places that are cluttered only by the occasional infatuations of architects, artists, clergy, and church members.

The lesson is this: The real testimony of function and effectiveness of any church is not to be found in its budget, its building, its membership list, or even its good works. The real testimony is in the invisible spiritual, emotional, mental, physical, familial, and conjugal crutches and casts that hang in its sanctuary, left there in gratitude by those who have been healed. Healed lives, healed hearts, healed homes—in all cases, healed souls—are the chief works of a church. The budget and the building, the membership list and the good works all are by-products (exceedingly important by-products though they may be) of those healings.

In the little rural church or the struggling neighborhood one, these spiritual crutches and casts may be almost visible. They take shape in the memory and knowledge of many members of the congregation. In a small church family, the healings are better known simply because the hurts have been better known.

In the large city church, with its loss of individual identity and interpersonal concern, it is usually only the pastor who knows the hurts and the healings, and there are many that even he never sees. Yet the hurts are just as painful, just as dangerous, when they are kept secret. Indeed, they are always more painful, more critical, when no one else cares.

The mink coat in the pew behind you and the overalls in the pew in front of you may cover souls and bodies that have been near to death, hearts that have been broken and made whole again, lives that have been rescued from disaster. There, in your modern building with its stone walls and bright glass or in your Victorian one with its Gothic oak, hang, if you could see them, testimonies to many human restorations and rescues, miracles of healing exceeding those of Lourdes.

If there are no such invisible crutches and casts in your church, then it is a sterile and useless place, without effect, without reality, no matter how good it looks in the annual report. But the chances are that the crutches and the casts are right there. And when the time comes that your heart is broken, your life is threatened, your soul is in need of the healing touch of Christ, your church is the place where you will find that touch, as have so many, so numberless many, before you.

42

AFTER THE HORSE
IS GONE

᭰᭣᭥᭡᭢

Allen and David stole apples from the supermarket. They
had been taught that stealing is wrong, and after they had
eaten the apples, they began to feel uncomfortable about
what they had done. They talked a little bit and agreed that
if they had some money, they would pay for the apples.

Allen continued to feel uncomfortable about it for a long
time. He felt kind of cheap when he thought about it, so
he tried not to think about it very often. He didn't like to
go near the market anymore because it reminded him, so
he found excuses not to run errands there for his mother.
Finally he forgot about the whole thing, or mostly. But he
didn't like apples much anymore.

David continued to feel uncomfortable about it, too. He
couldn't stand feeling that way, so he went to the market
and asked to see the manager. He wanted to crawl in a hole
when the manager walked in, but there wasn't any hole, so
he talked around a little bit about nothing much and finally
blurted out that he had stolen the apples.

The store manager asked him if he was sorry, and he said, "Oh, yes. You can bet I wouldn't be here right now if I wasn't. I can't pay for the apples, but I thought maybe you needed the front walk swept or something. I could do that."

David opened and unpacked cartons of canned goods for a while, and then the manager said he had a couple of apples coming. David really liked that store manager once he got over wanting to crawl in a hole. He liked the market, too, and he thought that perhaps next year he might be able to get a summer job there. And he still liked apples.

Allen and David both felt bad about the stolen apples. Allen felt remorse; David felt repentance.

43

FELLOW TRAVELERS

❧

A man who was hiking through an unfamiliar countryside came to a crossroad. There he had to decide which road he should take. There was a signpost, but just as he was about to consider it, another hiker came into view. The first traveler took off his pack and leaned against the post and waited for the second one to come within speaking distance.

"I was just wondering which road to take," he said. "I want to get to Winton. The signpost seems to point to Winton, I guess, but that road doesn't look like the one I expected somehow."

"No, indeed," answered the second hiker. "You are right to ask. You never can be sure about a signpost. That one has obviously been there for a long time and the road has undoubtedly been changed since it was put up. Besides, you can't really be sure it says 'Winton' because it is spelled with a Y instead of an I (if that's what it does say) and the N is worn off. You can't be quite sure what it is."

"Then, that's not the right road?"

"I'm sure that's not the road at all. Even if it does go to Winton, this other one will get you there much more quickly I should think. I'm going to take it. Come along with me."

The two travelers turned down the road that was not marked "Wynto. . ." on the signpost. When it began to get dark, the first man asked the second if he were sure they were going right and the other answered that of course he was.

By midnight, the first man knew that they were lost. Besides, he was hungry and tired and his feet hurt. The second man, however (rather doggedly, the first man thought), insisted the road was the right one.

At dawn they came at last to the end of the road. It ended in a field by a deserted farmhouse that could never conceivably have been Winton. The first man turned to the second one in anger at having been led astray.

"You really can't blame me," said the second man quickly. "After all, I'm only a traveler, too. How should I know any more about the roads than you do?"

Christians sometimes make the same mistake the first hiker made. They want to get to the city of joy and light that they've been told is waiting for them. They are traveling as hard as they can to reach the peace and fulfillment they have been told about.

There are signposts along the way. The signposts are old, sometimes older than recorded history, and sometimes the wording is archaic. Part of the directions have been lost by wear or neglect, but the meaning is still clear if you want to figure it out.

Yet there are so many people who tell them, "That is too old to be true. The details are inaccurate. Anyway the road doesn't look very inviting." But the people who say these things, no matter how confident they seem, no matter how up-to-date and how expert they are, cannot know the road one bit better than the struggling Christians who are far better off when they follow the old signs. For all the other people are traveling through this life for the first time, too.

44

WHICH DAUGHTER?

◆⸙◆

A woman lovingly packed her heirloom silver and sat down to decide which of her three daughters should have it. Amy would pack the silver away even more carefully than her mother had and would store it in a safe place, probably a bank vault. There the silver would stay. It would come to no harm, but neither would it come to anyone's sight. It would be the source of delight to no one. Amy would tell her friends about it, but she would never use it. She would be proud of it, but she would not enjoy it. It would be better, thought Amy's mother, housed in a museum.

Cornelia would use the silver, but she would enjoy it no more than Amy. She would use heirlooms as she used everything else, carelessly, thoughtlessly, unheeding. The silver would be thrown into the kitchen drawer with the steelware and used for anything from a Thanksgiving dinner to a country picnic. It would be better, thought Cornelia's mother, if it were melted down for the worth of the metal.

Elizabeth would care for heirlooms, but not anxiously. She

would use the silver, but not heedlessly. She would be proud of it, but would share it. She would be aware of its value, and also of its purpose. She would enjoy it. For what else, thought Elizabeth's mother, did it exist?

God isn't like the woman with the silver. He gives His gifts to all of us, but we treat His gifts very much as the three daughters would have treated the family sterling.

Some of us, perhaps most of us, are the Cornelia type. If we are, then we take the gifts of God so lightly that we forget that they ever were gifts at all and who has given them. We throw them into the clutter of a disordered and heedless existence and they are wasted. The Bible calls this throwing pearls in front of pigs. The Cornelia type stumbles over beauty without seeing it, treats its loves as casually as its acquaintances, and wastes intelligence and freedom, courage and faith on trivialities. Cornelias laugh at health and energy and throw them away.

Some of us, however, are the Amy type, treasuring God's gifts—and seldom using them. Amy people are so overwhelmed by the value of such gifts that they forget the purpose of them. Amys are too solemn to enjoy anything that concerns God, as if all of life were not God's concern. Parenthood, for this sort of person, is only a grim responsibility, and parents like that are either disastrous or dull. Amy people wring their marriages dry of all laughter, all true play, and in the end dry of all romance. To an Amy, vocation is neither a living nor a calling, but only an existence and a burden.

Those of us who are like Amy store our religion, courage,

and faith away where it can't be harmed, where it can't brush up against the rest of existence. We take such good care of our health that we forget what our bodies are for; we even put affection and love, and joy, away for "best."

Although they seem to be opposites, the Amy kind of person and the Cornelia type suffer from the same problem. They don't know how to treat the gifts of God because their concern is concentrated on themselves. Cornelia treats God's gifts lightly because nothing is important to her but Cornelia. It is really Amy that Amy takes so seriously, not the things that God has given her.

Elizabeth can really enjoy either heirlooms or the gifts of friends or the gifts of God because she has forgotten herself enough to see those things for what they are. Elizabeth, not Cornelia, really uses them, because she lets them serve their purpose. Elizabeth, not Amy, really knows their value. Elizabeth enjoys them and this is the first part of gratitude.

Whoever you are, whatever your lot in life, God has given you many things. How do you treat them? Christianity says that we must not only enjoy the gifts of God but that we are meant to enjoy God Himself, forever!

45

LOOKING FOR GOD

❧

If that familiar figure of fantasy, the being from another planet, were to have a good look around this world, he might go away as confused about us as we are about the possibility of his existence.

The Russian cosmonauts reported that they didn't find God in space. Our space being might report that he didn't find here any of the things we claim to have discovered and proved.

He could look through our biggest telescopes and never find a bacterium. He could look through our most powerful electron microscopes and never find a single star. He could search the greatest factories and find no geologic strata. At the bottom of the sea he would find no industry.

Sometimes we are as mixed up as that hypothetical creature and with less excuse. We try to find God through a telescope, and when He doesn't turn out to be a planet, we say He doesn't exist. A saint can find the signs of His presence in a planet, but you can only see God through a telescope if you have already found Him otherwise.

We try to find truth by looking through a microscope, and we have no luck at it. You can find facts by looking through a microscope, but truth is too big to slice up with a microtome and examine through a lens.

We look for faith in a laboratory, or in politics, or in the arts, and we don't find it. That doesn't mean that faith doesn't exist, nor does it mean that it doesn't work. It only means that we have looked in the wrong places.

If you want to know where to find God, ask the man who has already found Him. If you want the truth, look at a man who has given his life for it and to it. If you are looking for faith, find a man who loves enough to show it to you.

Maybe you don't really want to find any of these things because you have a sneaking feeling that if you found them, they might demand something of you. But you may come up against God someday, anyway, no matter where you look because, you see, *He* is looking for *you*, and He knows where you are. You may even find faith when you think you don't want it.

St. Paul did.

46

PUEBLO AND
PROJECT

◆§§◆

In the U.S. Southwest there is a highway that runs along
rugged mesas and fractured cliffs. It is an awesome area,
still breathing the unrest of the past when the mountains to
the west spewed forth liquid rock and white-hot ash and
formed the rocky cliffs. That mountain range was then one
great volcano, reaching high into the tormented sky. Now
even its long-dead skeleton speaks silently of ancient cataclysm.

It is a deserted country, but there are villages near. Some
of them are as empty and dead as the cold volcanic core—
the ruins of towns cut into the yellow cliffs by primitive
forebears of the modern Pueblo Indians. There are modern
Indian villages, too, themselves ancient and long outmoded
by the new century.

The twentieth century has not left this vast geographic
fossil untouched. There is one village there that has no ancient history. Most of its inhabitants are not Indian, and its

roots lie no deeper than a split atom. Los Alamos is the heart of the Atomic Research Project, and its inhabitants are men of the most advanced and modern technical and scientific knowledge.

Here is the other end of the stick, the antithesis of the antiquity and simplicity of the landscape and the pueblos. Yet these sophisticates are men very much like the Indian villagers; like the men who lived in the cliffs, they love and they hate, they hunger and thirst and tire, they strive for power. They wonder and they question and they die. The fires of nature still burn in their brains and the drums that beat in the pueblos centuries ago still beat in their veins.

The dead mountains nearby speak of cataclysm past, of the destruction and death that lie potential in the still-untamed force of the natural world. The bustling modern city speaks of cataclysm to come, of the destruction and death that lie potentially in the untamed force of man, who claims he can conquer the natural world.

From cataclysm to cataclysm, from destruction to destruction—this is the history of man's progress. He needs to do much more than harness nature; it is not enough for his safety that he should conquer the earth, if he ever does. Some men say sagely that the time has come when man must harness human forces, when he must conquer himself.

This he can never do. This progress, too, can only lead to destruction if he tries. Peace is not to be found in the Kingdom of Man.

If man would have human forces harnessed, if he would

be conquered by good, then he can only surrender to the God who created both the mountains and the men. Only God is big enough, or holy enough, to be trusted to handle such forces.

47

DOLLARS AND
DELPHINIUMS

❧

A young man sent a letter to his old uncle and enclosed some money. Remembering that his uncle was something of a gardener, he also enclosed a small packet of seeds from his prize delphiniums.

The old man had grown quite befuddled. He was happy to hear from his nephew but a bit out of touch with the practical realities of seeds and dollar bills.

"Put them in the bank," his housekeeper told him, thinking of the money.

"Put them in the ground soon," a friend told him, thinking of the seeds.

So it was that the old man got someone to take him to town one day and he carefully put the packet of seeds in his safety deposit box. He came home and dug a hole in the garden and put the money in it.

The delphiniums molded in the deposit box; the currency decayed in the ground.

A lot of people who still have all their faculties do much

the same thing. They bury the material, practical, immediate aspects of their Christianity in their inmost souls so that the very part of their faith that ought to be planted in the community to grow and bloom is instead left to disintegrate in the quiet isolation of their devotional life. But the part of their faith that belongs there, the part that should draw interest for eternal gain, they let rot unused and unuseful in the confines of this present world.

People plow under their impulses to compassion and honesty, to helpfulness and hospitality, and pile a foot of soggy emotion on top of them. Their self-discipline may be all wrapped up in little devotional rules and rituals or in negative rules of conduct, so that it never really sees the light of secular day. Their generosity gets tucked under the canned goods in the Thanksgiving basket and never finds its way into the cold reality of their conversation or their appraisal of other men and women. Their ethics lie smothered under ritual recitations of the Golden Rule, but they never show up in the office. For these people, religion is a sometime thing, and the sometime is always Sunday. The currency of their material Christianity is buried in the churchyard.

There are also people who confuse the bread of life with pie in the sky and will have none of either. These are they who think the only place to keep safe the seeds of everlasting life is the secular vault. They can conceive of no salvation outside social welfare. They are sure that if you love men (that is, if you feed or clothe or train them) you needn't bother about loving God. For them, silence is only wasted time, and prayer is wasted breath. They have faith only in activity; their hope is in utopia; their charity is given only to obvious need.

Christianity, like Christians, has both body and soul. It is both material and spiritual, outer and inner. The outer part of it is useless when it is buried. The inner part of it is wasted when it is not. Material Christianity must be circulated or it rots. Spiritual Christianity must be planted deep in the soul of man or it has no future.

Dollars are to be spent; delphiniums are to be planted.

48

THE BLUE GARDEN

❧

I remember once listening to a middle-aged enthusiast, the kind of a person who approaches everything in life with verve and élan. In fact that day her verve amounted almost to frenzy, as she asked advice from everybody as to how she should plant her garden.

She wanted a blue garden that year. She thought it would be striking, beautiful, and different. She dominated the conversation for a full half-hour with a discussion of what flowers could be had in shades of blue, how they would look together, what each needed in the way of sun and shade, moisture and fertilizer.

When, at length, she left, someone commented feebly that at least she had an interesting idea and that they would like to see the result. Said a woman who had known her for years: "Result? My dear, her potted geranium died last month because she forgot to water it."

There are more Christians than you might think who are like the woman who planned the blue garden. They undertake complicated Lenten projects. They schedule daily prayers involving the use of a half dozen manuals. They read scores of popular religious books and forget them. They read the Bible in five translations, or at least they intend to. They embark upon complex rules of life.

If you're one of these, go take a good look at your spiritual geraniums. God can make more use of one live potted geranium than of the loveliest of gardens that exist only in the planning stage.

49

FENCE STRADDLERS

Once there was a politician who was known for his ability to keep the admiration (and the votes) of the people on both sides of any question. He had made a career of well-timed fence-straddling.

One summer he joined a party of sightseers at the Grand Canyon. While they stood looking over the canyon, an argument developed. One man claimed that the north rim of the canyon was the more spectacular. Another claimed that the south rim was his choice. The politician's friend turned to him and pointed into the canyon. "Well, Jim," he said, "I'd like to see you straddle *that*."

The world is full of people who try to make a life out of straddling religious fences. Even the churches are full of them—people who try to have the best of both worlds, who try to be at home in the world and at the same time at ease in Christianity. They don't totally reject Jesus Christ, but they won't wholly accept Him. They admire Him very much, but they won't surrender to Him. They always take off their hats to Him, but they are never quite ready to fall on their knees before Him.

They would straddle the fence between the Christian claim, Christian commitment, and all the other ways of looking at life. The trouble is there isn't any fence there.

There is a canyon.

50

EMERGENCY ROOM

⋐§§⋑

The car coming toward you veers out of its lane into yours. Then there is horrible noise and worse pain, and you lie there, torn and bleeding and frightened. After what seems like a long time, an ambulance comes and takes you to the brightly lit assurance of a hospital emergency room. A surgeon comes in, gowned and scrubbed, to give to your injured body the help of his knowledge, his skill, and his experience.

The setting is dramatic, the figure of the surgeon is heroic, but the first thing he does is not a dramatic thing. It has more in common with housework than it does with heroism. He begins to clean out the wounds.

Carefully, painstakingly, sometimes even roughly, he sees to it that every bit of damaged tissue and foreign material that has found its way into those wounds is gotten out. Not until this apparently menial chore is done does he begin to cut and suture, to put into effect his knowledge of the location and function of muscles, nerves, and blood vessels.

He does this because if he didn't, foreign matter left deep

in tissue might set up infection and work widespread harm or arouse the body's natural rejective mechanisms. Without this cleansing, the results of the surgeon's work, even at best, will be marred.

The cleaning of a wound may seem routine, but it is an urgent matter. It is not enough in itself to bring about healing—not if the wound is a serious one—but still it has to be done before the healing can be helped to take place. The surgery may be intricate and expert, but first the debris has to be gotten out of the way. Indeed, debridement is the medical term for the process.

In the accidents that happen to us all on our journey through this life, at the times when we come suddenly and violently up against harsh reality, we get hurt. Sometimes we are badly hurt, and the wounds we sustain have to be expertly treated before they can heal. But even when the damage is not severe and a bit of bandaging is all we need, we have to take a lesson from the emergency room and get the debris out of the way first. We can wash out the little cuts and scrapes for ourselves, but our serious injuries need a skilled hand to be sure they don't heal with damaged flesh and dirt down inside to fester and threaten our health, maybe our lives.

For these wounds, God must be the surgeon. There is no other skilled enough, knowing enough, to suture the torn human spirit. But He does have His human assistants, and we must never be such snobs that we refuse the help of these members of His team—clergymen, family members, psychiatrists, friends, or maybe just people we happen to hear, who say what we need to have said or who do what we need to have done.

What kind of dirt gets down in the wounds that living inflicts, sooner or later, on most of us? What are the spiritual equivalents of the gravel and rust, the metal shards and broken glass that get into the physical wounds of a highway accident? They are many: the self-pity we feel at being hurt, the resentments, the blames we hold against other people for the part they play in our hurts (or the part we think they play), and the envies we feel toward those who don't hurt the way we do. They are the "if-only"s, too—the fantasies we repeat of acting differently in the past to avoid what we didn't avoid. They are the superstitions we indulge in when we think or feel that our suffering is punishment meted out to us by fate or by God. They are the shreds of normal self-centeredness that inevitably accompanies human pain, physical, emotional, or spiritual.

Men's spirits have built-in powers of self-restoration, much as their bodies have, but those powers, like the physical ones, are limited. The good surgeon's job is to do what must be done in order to give a broken body the chance to heal itself. So, too, there are things that must be done so that the human spirit can heal itself. First must come the debridement, getting the trash out of the wounds so that they can heal straight and without dangerous infection.

You don't clean out your own deep wounds while you wait for the ambulance. It is a painstaking job, requiring skill and objectivity. Spiritual debridement is not a do-it-yourself

128

undertaking either. You have to let the surgeon, let God, remove the potentially threatening things that have gotten inside you. Letting God do this is very much like letting the surgeon operate. It involves the same kind of giving up of yourself on the spiritual and emotional plane as is required when you let yourself be put on the table in the emergency room, when you give up your part in things and put yourself in his hands. When you are a victim of one of life's highway accidents, you have to be willing to put yourself into God's hands, to let God's team (whoever may be on it) carry and tend you, to let God pick out the debris that has gotten into your wounds. You have to turn over to Him the important doing of what needs to be done so that you can be made whole.